I0232814

How to Get Publicity for Your Book

NATALIE OBANDO

How to Get Publicity for Your Book
First Edition (2016)

Copyright © 2015 Natalie Obando

All rights reserved. No part of this publication may be
reproduced, stored in a retrieval system, or transmitted, in any
forms or by any means, without prior written permission of the
publisher

ISBN: 0997129603
ISBN-13: 978-0997129601

DEDICATION

To Grandpa Jojoe and Jujo.
Thank you for everything.

To writers everywhere, thank you for sharing
your stories.

CONTENTS

INTRODUCTION

I am living my dream life. My passion for books, reading, writing and news trends has turned into an amazing career. I received my BA in Journalism with an emphasis in public relations and a minor concentration in Creative Writing. This background has made it easy for me to always keep the creative in mind while still outfitting media needs. Over the past 8 years, I have been able to make a lucrative living off of not only reading books for free, but also telling others how great the books I read are. No, I am not a reviewer; I am a publicist. And it is my job to not only spread the word about books but also to get others to do the same.

Public relations is an intricate art form. Not only does it take a ton of time and dedication—one of the reasons I am paid to do this—it takes a thick skin, a way with words, and consistency.

In the years that I have been doing this whole PR thing, I have learned one rule: there is no one size fits all campaign, but there are plenty of PR practitioners who use the "one size" model for all their clients, which is sad really. I've seen so many authors that invest time, money, confidence, and trust into their publicists only to become just another account with the same tired campaign.

I am a big believer that your publicist should be your greatest champion. I am not saying that they need to constantly kiss your derriere, but they should whole-heartedly believe in your work and in you as an author. I'm not going to lie, I'm not the type of person to constantly praise someone, it's just not in my nature. But I am the type to relentlessly call and email an editor, producer, or reporter if I think that my client would be the perfect fit for their outlet. I don't blow smoke. I work hard, and in the ever-competitive world of media time, hard work and relentlessness are what matters.

I once had an author tell me she was a sensitive artist and that she needed a bit more praise from me: my response—get over it! As an author, be ready for people to criticize you, make fun of you, tell you how much you suck, and tell you that you shouldn't be a writer. You need to have a thick skin.

You should have the need to write because it's your passion and because you can't **not** write. If you are writing because you want to be famous or you want to write something that everyone loves, then I can honestly say that you should reconsider. Not everyone is going to love your work, nor are they going to praise you. That may feel bad at first but then there is that *moment* where someone tells you how your writing changed their life, and that is when all the negativity ever mentioned and all the naysayers disappear from that cloud above your pretty little head. That is the one moment that changes your life as a writer.

This book is my gift to hardcore writers. It is for those with the thick skin and right attitude. For those of you that know your work needs to be seen by others but might not know where to begin the path to doing so. Finishing your book is only a quarter of the battle. What lies before you after that final draft is ready for publication is a road that definitely needs some help in navigating.

If you know that you have what it takes to do it all on your own, then this book is for you. If you are savvy, pretty tech literate, social media shrewd, have time and a thick skin, then you can probably handle public relations for your author platform and your book. If you are confident in your work, there will never be anyone that can champion your book as much as you can.

CHAPTER 1:
THE TOOLS THAT YOU NEED

We will delve into these a bit deeper in the following chapters, but this is just to give you an overview of what the fundamentals are that you will need to actually be able to build and run your own publicity campaign for your book. This book was written for authors that have already done the things listed below or plan on doing do. These are non-negotiables. If you don't have these fundamentals down, then either acquire them or hire a PR agent that does. There is no point in trying to do your own publicity if these are not in place. It takes a skill set to be able to do it, and if you don't have the time or the skill, then either learn it before you attempt publicizing your work or hire a professional. The last thing you want to do is waste a reviewer's time or waste a producer's time. You also don't want to be known among media contacts as the author who always sends them things that aren't up to par with media and PR standards. Eventually they'll see your name and either toss it in the waste basket or mark you as spam.

Below are your non-negotiables...

A BOOK OR AN IDEA FOR A BOOK

Public Relations for an author doesn't need to begin once you've finished your book. It's actually a better idea to begin building your platform as an author before you even publish your book.

Are you a professional or expert that wrote or will be writing a book based on your expertise? Look for different outlets that you can contribute your knowledge to like magazines, blogs, news websites, etc. Are you writing a novel? Look for outlets that allow short fiction submissions or allow others to submit articles about their writing process.

Many agents will agree that it is important to have an established following as an author/ writer before submitting proposals to publishers, and that an established platform can actually help you get a contract with a publisher or agency.

If you don't have a finished product then make sure the concept is complete and outlined.

A PAID EDITOR

If you are self-publishing, then my advice to you is to make damn sure someone other than your BFF with great grammar skills edits your book. Save your BFF to be your beta reader. When it comes to editing your book and getting an editor, I'm talking about a professional. Yes, an editor that you will have to PAY to EDIT your work. Getting your book into the hands of the right editor is crucial. Let me lay it out for you, when you self-publish you are already fighting an uphill battle. ANYONE can self-publish these days. I have had more people than I can count want me to represent their self-published book and after I read it, I usually find spelling and grammar errors within the first couple of pages. I'm not saying that mistakes don't happen and I have seen some mistakes in traditionally published books, but the bottom line is that if you want critics to take a look at your book and give it a good review, the first step is in the editing. You can have the best story, characters, arc, or whatever—but if it is riddled with errors, people won't get past those.

Yes, it will cost money and yes, it might be pricey, but in the end, if you are going to put something out into the world and expect it to do well, then do what needs to be done to make sure that you put quality out and don't waste your time with something half-assed.

A BASIC UNDERSTANDING OF COMPUTER PROGRAMS

If you don't know what a Word document is or a PDF is, then start upping your computer vocabulary and understanding of different software. I hate to be the bearer of bad news, but we now live in a digital age. Programs are constantly evolving and you have to keep up. A well written email and well formatted PDF for your media kit will go a long way for reviewers and/or media contacts. If you can't put something together that looks nice, professional and has the right information, then you aren't going to get far and you will be wasting your time.

A BASIC UNDERSTANDING OF THE BOOK MARKET

As a writer you should try and immerse yourself in the publishing industry. Get to know the trade magazines as well as what current trends are going on in the market. Do you refuse to publish an EBook? Check out how EBook sales in your genre are doing. Do you want to solely stick to EBooks? Check out how print is doing in your genre. Everything is relative to your genre in this industry. There is no one size fits all plan for any book. So if you are planning on finishing or publicizing your book, make sure you know the ebb and flow of this crazy and exciting market.

A REALLY GOOD UNDERSTANDING OF YOUR GENRE AND READER MARKET

What category or categories of genre does your book fall into? What are some similar books that you can HONESTLY compare your book to? If you are writing YA but only read or know about the non-fiction self-help market, then that might not help your cause. Are sales declining in your genre? Who has had a successful publicity campaign with a book similar to yours? Can you point out some of the campaign points that drove awareness, sales and success? Knowing your competition and having someone that you look up to in your genre can help you take the right steps or avoid the wrong ones. Other than reading your genre of book, what do your target readers like to do? What are their hobbies, jobs, family status, sex, etc? Knowing your reader is critical to the success of your book.

A FUNCTIONING WEBSITE

This is your online presence. It is where readers, reviewers and producers will revert back to see who you are and what your book is about. Consider it an online résumé. It is the FOUNDATION of any PR campaign so make sure yours is stellar! With the website templates that are now available on WordPress, Wix, Squarespace, and Weebly, creating your own website doesn't have to be expensive. Even if you need to hire someone to do this, you can get a really nice website for a price anywhere from $500 to $2000, depending on the content and design.

A PRESENCE IN AND KNOWLEDGE OF SOCIAL MEDIA

Do you know what a Twitter handle is? Do you know the difference between a Facebook author page and a personal Facebook page? Social media is AMAZING, crazy, evolving, and the best tool for an author to connect DIRECTLY to his or her reader. As an author with a crazy writing schedule, it may be hard to keep up with the ever-changing social media Joneses, but it is a big part in gaining a wider audience. Knowing which social media platforms are best for you and your book can help you hone in on your audience and also help you to better understand at least one social media platform. This is another aspect of a campaign that I recommend hiring someone to teach you about. If that is not an option, I also recommend watching free online tutorials to help you understand the ins and outs of social media. Social media is now a staple in our society and a staple in any campaign.

TIME AND PATIENCE

If public relations were easy-peazy, then I would be out of a job. It takes time, patience, and know-how. I can help you understand what you need, but you need to make the time for it. You also have to understand that everyday journalists are being bombarded by hundreds of authors or people that think their story is the next best thing that should get coverage from them. Self-publishing has made it easier for everyone to get their story out, but that just means there is a lot more competition. Even if your book does get requested by a reviewer or producer, it doesn't necessarily mean that they will cover it. Make sure you have the patience and time to fully dedicate to your book's PR efforts.

A THICK SKIN

When you send reviewers pitches, you might not hear back, you might hear no, and you might hear yes and then see a review that says the book was horrible. Be realistic. You can't please everyone and trying to will only hurt you even more. All the negatives don't mean that you're a bad person, that you aren't smart, or that you are a bad writer, it just means that you aren't the writer for them, or that your book wasn't for them. Don't take things too personally. A real writer writes because they have to, it's in their blood and a few people with negative opinions about them will never stop that.

CHAPTER 2:
YOUR ONLINE PRESENCE

Why You Need A Website And What It Should Include

A personal or book website is your stamp on the World Wide Web. True there are billions of sites out there, but we live in a society where people want things at the speed of light and if they can't get it, they forget it. As an author, it is imperative that you have a presence online other than your social media, because your book is your BUSINESS, and you are trying to sell yourself as an author and sell your book.

Your website is where readers, fans, reviewers, publishers, other authors, and every media contact you try and connect with can quickly and easily find out more about your writing, your style, and what you have to offer versus the millions of other authors.

And it's not enough that you just have a website. You have to make sure that you have a professional-looking site if you want to be taken seriously by all of the above.

What I mean by professional is not just your run-of-the-mill WordPress blog, but an actual site with various pages structured in an organized fashion.

YOUR URL AND SOCIAL MEDIA LANDINGS

I have met so many authors that have an array of names and titles to all their different social media and websites. I understand that perhaps you have a business that you started before the book and want to drive traffic there, or that you want to highlight your business, or whatever it may be, but I must warn that it is imperative to have your URLs and social media sites be consistent with your product.

This means that if your website is dogoodprgroup.com, then your social media should be facebook.com/dogoodprgroup and your Twitter should be @dogoodprgroup and your Instagram should be @dogoodprgroup, etc. You get the picture, right?

If you have many different types of genres and books that you are selling or promoting, I suggest not using titles of books for your website and instead, use your name. That's right, brand **yourself** and in doing so you can promote all your work in one central hub.

It is important that your audience know that they only have to go to one hub to easily find all of your work. This way there is no confusion. The easier you make it to find all your work, the easier you make it to BUY all your work.

Having the same URL and social media information also makes it easier for media to get ahold of you or search you. Keep this in mind when choosing what they will be. While unique is great, you have to make sure that you are able to brand yourself with that uniqueness, and if you don't have the dedication to do so, then all it will do is confuse your fan base and potential media.

PAGES ON YOUR SITE

There should be about 4-6 different pages on the website of an author that is just starting out. These include a home page, book/s page, about the author page, a contact page, and you can add a media page and a blog page as your book gets more coverage and you create content. Before you begin setting up the site, make sure you have all the content and copy for your site. Do NOT get all frilly with the site and try to make it overly flowery with your Creative Writing chops. Instead, make sure you look at it from a reviewer/media standpoint. Media people tend to want the facts with a hint of your personality; it's the journalist in them. So get your copy/content ready and make sure you have the items listed below for your website.

Links to buy the book

There should always be a link that your website visitors can easily see that directs them to a place where they are able to purchase the book online. If possible make it available via different vendors such as Barnes & Noble,

Amazon, Book Bub, Indie Bound, IBooks, Google Play, Kobo, etc. You don't have to use all of those sellers, but you should try and have more than one option for buying the book to make it easier for the buyer. Also, some of these selling platforms are more popular in other countries so it makes the book available globally. The ultimate goal is to sell as many books as possible and to make it as easy as possible to purchase them.

I recommend that you have links to buy the book at the top of each page on your site. Always make it easy for a reader to buy. Never require your website visitor to search your site for a place to buy the book. Position buy buttons on your page in easy to see places. Buy buttons work best if they are subtle but in plain sight. They should be something that must be glanced at when your eyes scan the page. If they are obnoxiously big or too distracting, then it may seem like you only care about selling your book, but if they are subtle and easy to see and use, then your reader will see that you want to connect and also make it easy for them to purchase the book. Having subtle buy links on every page keeps the possibility of buying the book in mind for your potential reader.

HOME PAGE

Your "Home Page" should have things that highlight all of your work. Whether it be great reviews, a book trailer, a recorded interview, a slider of different images from the events that you held, a slider of images that relate to the book with quotes from the book or reviews imposed on the image, or whatever it is that you know will give the reader a feel for the book and you, the author. If you have more than one book it should have all of your books on the home page so people can get a sense for your writing style and collective work.

What I tend to do for authors that are just starting out and have one book is make the "Home Page" which is the landing page a place that summarizes everything— from whom you are to what type of book you are promoting. It can be a welcoming of sorts that greets the reader and sets the tone for you as an author. Your landing page should always be your "Home Page". I have seen people who have pages that are somewhat of an intro page, but then you have to choose to enter the site, which is an unnecessary added step for people to have to go through to find out more about the book and you. You should also have all the links to your social media accounts along with the widget at the top of each page to make it visually appealing and easy for people to click over to your social media. Each link should ALWAYS open in a separate tab. You never want your links to direct the reader completely away from your website to another site and not have it easy to get back to, and by easy, I mean, still up on your browser.

AUTHOR PAGE

This page should have your professional bio. Notice I wrote BIO and NOT résumé. It should have a professionally written history of you and your writing in a story-like form. It should never be a list of your accomplishments, but rather, a captivating mini-story about yourself. You can choose to do it in either first or third person. And if you want it to be a bit more personalized, you can also add information about yourself that doesn't have to do with writing. If you were awarded something in your professional field and this award shows a level of your intelligence, then go ahead and mention it. Truth be told, this is pretty much a tactfully written "brag" page.

Author Picture on Your Author Page/Bio

You should definitely have professional author photos taken. A good headshot can sway an opinion about an author. The old saying, "Don't judge a book by its cover" was made up, because we tend to do exactly that as humans— judge something by the way it looks. So if you have a photo that is poorly lit and you look like a mess, then people might not take you as seriously as an author whose photo looks neat and whose picture pops. The color of clothes, lighting, and background can send a message to your reader about you without them even knowing it. Are you writing a book about some sort of professional field? If you are, you better look the part. Dressing and looking the role is a measure of your credibility. I am definitely not saying to jump into a suit and look stiff, but you want your personality to shine through all your work and information about you, and that includes your author picture.

BOOK(S) PAGE

Besides talking a bit about your book on your home page (or if you have more than one book, talking about the latest book or most current news about your books), you should have a full page dedicated to your book. If you have more than one book, then you should have a page for each. For multiple books, you should have a "BOOKS" tab that has a drop down menu with the title of each book on that drop down menu that you are able to click on and have the site take you to each specific book page.

The "Book Page" should have the title of the book as the header as well as the buy links. Yes, again with the buy links, so that people can buy the book, should be all over your site, tastefully. You don't want to make the mistake of having your potential fan/reader "search" for your book.

MEDIA PAGE

Once you've finished reading this book, you should be ready to get some media attention, so make sure you have a page dedicated to your reviews and mentions. Post links to all of your reviews, guest articles, op-eds, guest blogs, interviews, etc. on the media page. If there are print articles that you or your book(s) are featured in, make sure to put those on the media page as well as a downloadable PDF with an introduction to each right above the link or download button. Consider adding a downloadable PDF of your book's press release or any other press releases to this page that you think are of interest to media outlets. Think of this part of your website as your résumé and references for potential media. If editors/reporters/reviewers see that you have constant coverage, it shows that you are still a timely subject, and that you are newsworthy.

CONTACT PAGE

This is probably the easiest page that you will build on the site, because it has the least amount of content. Nevertheless, it still needs to be clear as to how you can be reached. I always suggest that you use a contact form. Most WordPress and other website templates come with a premade contact page that you can simply insert into your website. This type of page typically allows your site to filter out spam because the contact form requires that the viewer leave their information so that you may respond to them at your convenience. It also keeps your personal information off of your website but still allows readers access to you.

BLOG PAGE

Blogging on topics that pertain to your book or writing is important for an author. We all want to be seen as experts and influencers in our field. The more you know and share with your fans and colleagues, the more of an influencer you will become. But do make sure that you are writing and blogging about topics that you REALLY know about.

Many of the fiction authors that I work with tend to not want to write about things other than their book, because they don't consider themselves experts in anything other than their books. To that, I say that it is totally fine to write about insight into their characters (especially if they appear in more than one book), but your readers and fans also see you as an expert in writing. A blog post about your writing process, how you approached a publisher, or even about how you got published could be exactly what inspires your readers.

Also, keep in mind that providing content for your blog page also boosts the search engine optimization (SEO) for your site and helps to drive more traffic to your online platform.

PUTTING IT ALL TOGETHER

Think of your website as the home of your online presence. Sure, there are definitely going to be other online platforms that you will be using, but your website is what brings them all together. The online world can be a bit scattered, and you need a place that hones them all in for the sake of your readers, editors, producers, event coordinators, and anyone else you are approaching to help you promote your book. It may seem like a lot now, but once your website is in place, it will make your life easier.

Reference:

Most of the authors I work with aren't necessarily web designers, so here are a few sites that offer premade themes/templates (page designs) for websites that are fairly easy to use:

http://www.wix.com/website/templates

http://www.squarespace.com/templates

http://themeforest.net/category/wordpress

CHAPTER 3:
SOCIAL MEDIA

Why You Need It And How To Use It Effectively

I could probably write an entire book on this one subject, but for the sake of time management and for the sake of giving you exactly what you need, I won't bore you with all the intricate details. But you do need to know this: IT IS ESSENTIAL THAT YOU HAVE A SOCIAL MEDIA PLATFORM!

Get over your phobias and get over yourself. We are in the Digital Age. In a few years, Millennials will make up over 70% of the buying market, and you need to connect with them. Remember when you thought that you didn't need email? Remember when you thought that the Internet was a fad? I might be giving away my age, but I do.

Look, I KNOW that social media can be intimidating, but social media is what is occupies the mindless pastimes of many. It is a way people get information. It is a way people connect. It is a way people brag. It's where some people form social opinions. It is the present and the future.

Think of all your favorite media outlets, TV and radio shows, etc. They probably ALL have some sort of social media. This is the new way to disseminate information. And it is a way for an author to DIRECTLY connect with their readers or potential readers.

Now, believe me, I was hesitant in embracing this whole social media thing too, but it isn't just a "social media thing" anymore. It is a way of communication. There are entire courses, classes, even degrees that delve into this new addition to society and culture. I equate social media to the telephone as far as its life-changing impact on the way we link up with people.

So, first things first: what social media platforms should authors use? Well, there are a plethora to choose from, but let's start with the basics and work our way through the ones with the most impact.

FACEBOOK

Facebook is a platform that allows you to share text, images, videos, and links to other articles/sources of information. It is a must for ALL authors. The need for a Facebook account is similar to the need of having an email address; you just have to have it in order to communicate with the most people. So if you are going to start with any social media platform, let it be

Facebook. This social media platform also has the most active users. It has approximately 1.5 billion monthly active users where other sites are still just in the millions.

The translation between Facebook users and book buying is also great. More than 70% of Facebook users are book buyers, which means that you have a great chance at connecting with and engaging with new readers and fans.

Facebook is also used by an older demographic, so that might be something to think about when thinking of how to connect with your target audience. Is your book geared toward Baby Boomers? Well, then chances are that if they are any social network at all, then they are on Facebook.

When starting and building a Facebook page for your book or work as a writer, keep a few things in mind:

> You should decide whether you want an author page or a book page.

>> A book page would be a wise idea if you plan on only writing one book, or if the book title is catchy and relates to a cultural phenomenon. It is also a good idea if you plan on writing a series of books with the same title but a different subtitle. If you plan on writing various books on completely different marketable ideas then this might be a better option for you but maintaining many platforms is hard work. Most

of the time, I suggest that my authors steer clear of this approach and rather than build a book page, I suggest that they build an author page.

An author page is best if you plan on writing more than just one book, and also if you plan on doing something in the literary industry (IE editing manuscripts for others, teaching a writing workshop, blogging about writing).

I consider having an author page as a step to branding yourself and all the work you have produced or will produce rather than branding just one book or a series of books with the same title.

Either one you choose, you will have to have a personal page to access either one. There are many free step-by-step tutorials online that will help you begin this process. Many are video tutorials, and there are also many books and free literature online that can help you do this. You just have to dedicate the time. I also provide a free step-by-step tutorial on my website www.DoGoodPRGroup.com/facebook.

Once you have this set up there are other things to consider:

Who is your target audience for you current work?

You must consider this when deciding what to post for your content. You want to post content that appeals to your target demographic. So, what I mean by this is if your target demographic is women ages 30-40 who are looking for love, then you probably don't want to post information about the latest football game stats or the latest hotrod car. Sure, some of your target readers might care about this, but the whole point in having a Facebook page is to share information that is relevant to your work and book. You want Facebook users to know that your Facebook page is a source of relevant information pertaining to your book or the topics that you write about. This is the first step towards branding your work.

An example would be if you write about dating and relationships, then it might be a fun idea to have information about the single life. It could be statistics on the state with the most single people, a Top 10 List of the Best Places to Meet Someone, or an inspirational quote about finding love. Whatever it may be, make sure it pertains to your work. Sure, once in a while, it could be fun to change things up a bit, and that's fine, but make sure you don't deviate too often or else people won't know what direction you are going.

What type of content should you post on Facebook?

When you have a public page, it becomes increasingly more difficult to get organic views of the content that you share. What does this mean? It means that the people over at Facebook aren't sharing your content the way they used to. Less and less people are seeing posts, but the good news is that they are still seeing them, and anyone can go to your page if they choose to seek out the content you are sharing. For this reason, you should be very choosy as to what you are sharing. People aren't going to care what you are having for breakfast every morning; UNLESS you are a dietician, or your book is about health, diet, etc. Furthermore, some people use social media to gripe about things and to this I say, DON'T. Unless you are starting a movement against something or actively trying to change something, don't use Facebook as a place to complain about things. People already have complaints of their own; they don't need to see more.

A Facebook page for an author should share mixed media: text, pictures, video, and website article links. Some ideas would be text quotes from your book, pictures from places or things that you are doing to promote your book or riveting pictures that associate with the topics of your book, fun pictures of you writing on vacation, website links to articles that have to do with your book or industry, videos that have to do with your book topic that are from other platforms, videos that you made yourself as a part of a tutorial of your book topic, a book trailer, etc.

How often should you post content?

Content is king nowadays. There is such an abundant amount of content available to readers or perusers of social media that you must continue to post to stay relevant, especially if you are a first time author. If you aren't yet getting spots on morning news shows or in newspapers, the only other way to have you and your work continually in front of readers is through Facebook (and other social media) postings. For this reason, I recommend that you post daily. If that is just too much for you then post at least two to three times per week and make sure that you engage in those posts. Meaning, if someone comments on the post, respond and have a conversation that is light, fun, informative, but most importantly, it shows you care about what they say.

How personal should it be?

Let's stick with old school decorum and just say, never discuss religion, politics, or anything a little too personal unless the discussion is non-biased and has to do with the book you are promoting. If your book is overtly biased on one of these topics, then, by all means, go ahead and post your political opinions if you are trying to segregate your market and are really trying to connect with those that see that point. Most people love to connect with an author on a personal level, but they also appreciate an author (especially a first-time author) who is open-minded and doesn't force their opinions down their throat but rather lays issues in front of them in a very diplomatic way. Again, if your book is about doing the first, then chances are that you can get away with it.

What pictures should I post? How do I make pictures for my Facebook that market my book?

Everything that you post should be to either directly or indirectly sell your book. This doesn't mean that you have to constantly ask people to buy your book, but it does mean that postings should have that in mind. Your Facebook cover image should have the picture of your book(s), the release date, where it's available, and/or pictures of all your books.

A really great place to make cover pictures that have preset templates for Facebook is Canva. If you have a great knack for design but not for

Photoshop, another great website is Picmonkey for an easy way to put your eye for design into play.

www.canva.com

www.picmonkey.com

Facebook users like to see images that connect with them or take them to where they want to be. It is quite all right to connect with your Facebook followers on a personal level by posting a picture of you on a cool vacation or you doing something awesome that might inspire others to do something similar. It is also okay to post pictures of daily things that connect with the book or your work. Did you have a successful book launch or school visit? Post some pictures! But unless you are writing a book about fitness, refrain from posting too many pictures of yourself that are self-taken, which are more commonly known as "selfies." Some people find it to be a little egocentric, and I am one of those people. So unless you are doing something really awesome that requires you to take a picture of yourself doing it, just don't. The only time selfies are somewhat acceptable are if you are writing a book about weight loss and are documenting it via before and after pictures and sharing that with your readers. Also, if you happen to be in a situation that shows you are doing something interesting that people might want to know about and don't have someone to take the picture for you, then that's okay too. As a general rule, I tell my clients, if you would feel weird asking a stranger to take a picture of you doing whatever it is that you are doing, then don't post it on Facebook as a selfie. For instance, would you ask a coffee shop employee to take a picture of you looking down at your computer writing? Probably not, right? So don't take a selfie doing so.

Many of the most successful Facebook posts I have seen were pictures with quotes or statistics from books, authors, and experts on top of them. Posts like these have two elements: first, we have a visual element (the picture) that connects with the Facebook follower right away, meaning the viewer doesn't have to read the post to already connect to something. The second is the text or information which retains the viewer's attention for a bit longer allowing them to connect with it on a completely different level. The more a viewer connects with a post, then the more they will share it. For instance, would you rather show your friends a nice picture of someone they don't know or a picture of a setting with an inspirational quote on it? I'm going to guess you said the latter. Odds are someone who doesn't know that person won't connect with the first picture. But they have two ways of connecting with the other, visually and verbally.

The point of making these posts is to try and get as many organic shares as possible. Meaning that people who see the post will share it on their wall, then their Facebook friends will share it on their walls and so on and so forth. When Facebook users share your posts, you are now dipping into their audience/friend pool, and if the post is compelling or share-worthy enough, people will go back to the source (your Facebook page) to see what else you have that might be worthy of sharing to their friends.

What else should I post?

Well, if we are talking about Facebook, then let's get into some new things that are happening over there. Facebook is now making it easier and much more worthwhile to share videos. It can be a video you make from your laptop, a part of a webinar series that you are in, a video interview, or a video made on your phone. Whatever way you made it doesn't really matter as long as the quality of the video (meaning the picture) is good and the content is GREAT!

You want to post videos that compel people to do things. Whether it be to start writing themselves or to go buy your book, your video should be a way for your followers to see you in action and connect with you on a more personal level because you are there in front of them emotions and all, and they can really see how passionate you are about what you do.

Some great examples of video social media marketing are Tastemade videos as well as Buzzfeed videos. Now obviously, these are videos that are professionally produced, but if you look at some of the ones shared on Tastemade's Facebook page, they are amateur but the quality of the video looks good enough. More importantly is that they stir an emotion in you that only video can.

For more Facebook information, I offer a guided tutorial for Facebook on my website at www.DoGoodPRGroup.com/facebook.

TWITTER

Twitter is another great marketing tool for writers and helps you to be concise and to the point because of their word count/character regulations. Twitter only allows you to use 140 characters so you have to make sure that you are using them all in the most efficient way as possible. That does not mean 140 words; it means 140 total uses of space. Twitter tends to be a quick way to get a ton of information. Your Twitter feed is constantly moving (depending on how many people you are following), and there tends to be more use of hashtags on Twitter than on Facebook. Twitter also has less ad appearances, so many people favor Twitter because of this.

What is nice about Twitter and Facebook is that you can directly link them so that you don't have to constantly update your feed on both. The only downfall to this is that if you link your Twitter feed to your Facebook feed you will not receive full images from Facebook to Twitter (as of February 2016), only a link back to Facebook which some Twitter users may not have or which some people may not want to click on to see the whole post. It is definitely more convenient to link the two, but it is recommended to vary your posts slightly so that people on your social media have a slightly different experience every time.

Gaining Twitter Followers

> Twitter is a helpful tool to gain an audience as long as you maintain audience expectations. Meaning, you should post consistently and engage often. Make sure that you are connecting with the people who are following you and looking at and sharing their content. The more people see that you share their stuff, the more they will share yours.

So how do you gain these followers to engage with them? Simply start following people that you think will follow you back. It might be difficult to gauge this at first but after a while, it will become elementary. It is safe to say that a blogger who reviews books similar to what you write is a good person to follow, because they might have a following of people who like your type of book. It is also safe to say that this person might be inclined to follow you since you write about topics that they enjoy.

If you decide to follow people who are famous or high profile in hopes that they will follow you, chances are they won't unless you have some very witty or interesting posts that they can see when they get the notification that you are a new follower. My suggestion is to start from the core of who your fan base is and grow from there.

For a full Twitter tutorial visit www.DoGoodPRGroup.com/twitter.

INSTAGRAM

I used to think that Instagram was for the super vain, because it was riddled with people posting selfies, but I've changed my tune quite a bit in the past year. Instagram is a completely visual social media platform and a great way to get your message across visually.

What this means is that the more creative you are to get your message across through an image, the more you are likely to get followers and engagement. Whereas on Twitter, it is all about how witty you can be in those 140 characters that you have to use; on Instagram, it is all about how visually appealing your content is in their format. Some authors that I have worked with didn't feel the need to have an Instagram account until they started one and saw how quickly their followers added up and also, the great engagement that they received if they posted visually appealing posts. Although Instagram still is a newbie to the social media game and has fewer users than Facebook or Twitter, a recent study done by the research company Forrester showed that Instagram is the leader in social media engagement across all platforms. This has been true from 2014 and 2015 although the numbers dropped a bit in 2015.

Some of the most successful authors that I have seen use Instagram are authors of cookbooks, motivational authors, fitness authors, business authors, etc. People seem to need a strong motivational force daily, so if you can leverage that need in your posts, chances are you can connect with a wide audience. Also, if you can visually show someone how to do something then they have a better chance at doing it correctly.

If you are an author and fitness coach, there is a good chance that your audience wants to see you perform an exercise that might sound a little tricky in a book, but if you can walk them through it in a 10 second video, then it will help and motivate them to succeed.

For more information about Instagram visit www.DoGoodPRGroup.com/instagram.

HOOTSUITE IS YOUR NEW BESTFRIEND

I would die without Hootsuite. Not literally, but my brain would explode when it comes to all this social media upkeep. And let's be realistic, it takes a lot of time and energy to maintain this all. To be honest, I slip from time to time, because we are always so busy here maintaining our client's social media platforms and that's okay. Sometimes you just have to forgive yourself and move on. But what I have found that has made my life a lot easier in terms of social media management is Hootsuite, which allows you to control all of your social media platforms—and for us, the platforms of clients that we are working on— from one space and allows scheduling, tracking, monitoring and measuring; making it a whole lot easier to maintain your platforms without pulling out all of your hair.

Hootsuite is accessible via your smartphone and will let you know before it posts something so that you may approve it before it goes live, which is helpful if you have others helping you run your social media platforms and you want to approve postings before they go live.

If you find that getting in one zone helps you with social media, then Hootsuite is a great tool for you. It has all of your platforms visually side by side so that you can see what is going on in real time.

I love and recommend it, but there are other social media management tools that you can use as well like TweetDeck or Social Engage. There are many, but I think that Hootsuite really works across so many different platforms and provides such great measurements and analytics for authors that it is my go-to and what I recommend.

FINAL THOUGHT

Once you have set everything up and are comfortable posting, ask yourself who have you spread the word to so far about your book? Are you reaching out to other writers? If so, then your book should help them with their writing. Make sure that you are reaching out to people or groups who are going to spread the word about your book. These would be the bookworms that you know, book lovers, book clubs, librarians, book reviewers, and avid readers. Always keep that audience in mind when reaching out.

Social media isn't just about asking for stuff like reviews or just for building your social presence, but it's also about paying it forward in the social media world. Would you like it if another author shared your book information? Would you like it if someone reposted, shared, or retweeted something that you shared on your social media? Of course, you would! So do it for others as well. Share their posts to your network, retweet or favorite the tweets that you like. You never know what type of friendships or alliances you'll make and chances are, they'll pay it forward as well.

CHAPTER 4:
YOUR BOOK ON AMAZON

The number of people who buy their books from Amazon has surpassed those that buy their books from brick and mortar stores as well as other online retail platforms combined; not just for e-books but for print as well. According to an article in *Forbes*, the proportion of all books sold in the U.S. that are Kindle titles is 19.5%. E-books make up around 30% of all book sales, and Amazon has a 65% share within that category with Apple and Barnes & Noble accounting for most of the balance. Amazon is such a leader in the book world that it boasts its own imprint and is also looked to as a scale of success for authors. The titles "New York Times Bestselling Author" and "Amazon Bestselling Author" both carry a great if not equal amount of clout in the book world today. Having your book ranked as a top seller in certain Amazon categories is also a great feat and means sales.

Making sure that your book is available on Amazon is essential for sales and the platform that Amazon provides for authors is easy to use and extremely beneficial.

Most publishing houses will add your book to Amazon to sell on your (actually their) behalf, but many won't take advantage of their free author platform that houses an official author page for you to add an RSS feed from your blog, videos, host your live Twitter feed, showcase your author bio, and allows you to post upcoming author events. Taking advantage of this free platform is a must and only takes a few minutes to update.

Your Amazon author page allows you to have another platform and makes you that much easier to search not only in Amazon but also online. It also gives readers who are looking at your book a little more background on who you are and what other books that you have written without leaving the Amazon hub which just makes it easier for them to shop your books.

It is, of course, a great idea to take advantage of other hubs where you can sell your book, but none are as vast as Amazon. I can't tell you how many times I have been shopping on Amazon for something other than a book and have wandered over to the books page and snatched one up just because it looked interesting.

Amazon is a leader in sales and is constantly being perused by buyers so make sure that you set up your Amazon platform because it's where most of the world's book buyers go to get their books.

CHAPTER 5:
GOODREADS: A "READER TARGETED" SOCIAL MEDIA PLATFORM

Due to the overwhelming nature of the Web, there is a lot to learn about how to use social media to best promote your book, so I didn't include Goodreads in Chapter Two. But it is a social media platform, and a GREAT one, deserving of its own chapter.

When Goodreads first came out, I couldn't have been happier as my inner (sometimes outer) geek marveled at all the books that I could chat about in discussion forums and all the books that I would soon discover.

Goodreads is not only what I expected it to be, but it also blew up into the Facebook for readers. What I mean by that is that it is the biggest social media platform exclusively for those with an interest in books! You can't get any better than that!

Authors and readers alike can join forums, talk about their books, set up author chats, host giveaways, and recommend books to their friends. It's easy, it's interactive, and it is free.

Not only can you set up a profile as a user, but you can also set up an author profile and later merge the two.

Setting up an author profile on Goodreads helps to further promote yourself as an author and also helps you interact with an audience that you already know are your target.

Other forms of social media have a vast and diverse audience making it a lot tougher to pinpoint the readers and your targets (this can be done on Facebook, but it takes time and you have to use target paid ads and paid posts), but Goodreads actually has groups that make it easy to identify your targets and reach out to them. Do you have a book about zombies? There is a group for zombie fans. Do you have a book about female superheroes? There is a group for Fangirls. There is pretty much a group for everything; you just need to reach out and tap in.

Goodreads was designed for readers, so if you know your reader, then it is easy to interface with them without being pushy.

There is a tutorial for authors on Goodreads that can be found here:
https://www.goodreads.com/author/how_to

This is a great tutorial and will give you the gist of how of use it. If you know how to use Facebook then Goodreads will be easy. So dive into it and check out all the great opportunities.

CHAPTER 6:
GETTING YOUR CAMPAIGN STARTED
WITH PRE-PUBLICATION REVIEWS

At this point you should have all your ducks in a row:

- Your website is looking great and conveys your personality
- Your social media platforms are up and running, and you are engaging daily with your followers
- You book is thoroughly edited is ready to be published

And now you need pre-publication reviews...

Getting your book reviewed prior to it being published is a lot easier than trying to do so after the book has been published and has been on sale for a while. This isn't impossible, but it takes a lot more time and tact to do so. Reviewers typically want books that are brand new, and chances are brand new means 3-6 months in advance of the book being published. This is a general rule of thumb for bigger publishing houses. And while for some publishing houses the book may not be complete (cover isn't designed, needs a final editing, etc.), it is noted that it is an "Advance Reviewer Copy" or a "Galley."

When reviewers see that they have this copy rather than the finished product they know that mistakes are possible and allow for that, but most of the book should be complete.

WHY GET A PRE-PUBLICATION REVIEW?

Pre-publication reviews not only help set the tone for your book campaign and encourage other reviewers to read it later in the campaign, but they also get your book on bookstore and library radar early on. Bookstores place their orders early with bigger publishers based on a catalog or from their sales reps, and these catalogs and sales reps sell the book by using pre-publication reviews to show buyers that the book is well-written, well-liked, and will sell.

But a pre-publication review can't come from just anyone. They have to come from reputable sources. As an author with a larger publishing house, you will find that the publishing house will take care of acquiring these pre-publication reviews for you because their goal is to sell your book. As an author published by an indie publishing house, you might be able to attain these as well, but some indie houses just don't have the budget to work on this or acquire these for your book. But as a self-published or hybrid published author, it is all up to you.

I work with some really reputable pre-publication reviewers and have many listed on my site. If you would like to check out some of the ones that I recommend go to www.DoGoodPRGroup.com/pre-pub-reviews. Below are some of my standard go-to's:

Kirkus Reviews
This is a professional review group and one of the most trusted sources for indie author reviews. It's also one of the most pricey, but you can get a discount if you go to my website: www.DoGoodPRGroup.com/kirkus.

Foreword Reviews
This review group is reputable and gives objective reviews with a readership of mainly librarians and booksellers as well but it takes quite some time to find out if your book has been chosen for review and because of their space limitations, they're only able to review 150 books per issue of their quarterly magazine. If you aren't willing to wait a month to know *if* your book was chosen for review or if it wasn't chosen for review, then they have a subsection for indie and self-published authors that is a great source for a review, see below.

Clarion Reviews
This is the subset of Foreword reviews that most clients tend to use , as it is less costly and also very timely. They have a great express delivery option of 4-6 weeks, which really helps when you are crunched for time (although you still have to plan for this).

San Francisco Book Review/Manhattan Book Review

There is a 90-day timeframe on this, so you have to make sure that you send your book to them early on. If you accidentally let time lapse, there is a paid option; generally if you plan well, you can get your book reviewed here in a timely fashion. If you do happen to use the pay option to guarantee the review and the review isn't favorable, you can choose to purchase an ad on the site instead, which is great. I especially like this review group, because they have a dedicated children's section and children's online magazine that hosts video reviews by children for children. It is not only really adorable, but it connects you to that target market emotionally.

Midwest Book Review/California Bookwatch

These two review groups are one in the same; they are not fee-based and generally have a very fast turnaround time for books that they accept. They generally take about 3-6 weeks. I really like to use them, because they are free and have a great reputation.

While some of these are fee based, others are not but you have to wait for your book to be chosen to be reviewed which can take a while and if you want the review before the publishing date, I suggest picking, at least, two of these review sites for your reviews. They are the most reputable, objective and have the best turnaround time.

A great rule of thumb is to take a look at the books that they have reviewed that are similar to what you have written—genre, author writing style, topic, etc. Once you have decided on which one works best for you, simply follow the submission guidelines on each website.

Other review sites are available for reviews for your book, and there are also quite a few free reviews that you can acquire, but for the purpose of pre-publication reviews, they might not be the best choice due to the turnaround time. Many of the free reviewers are inundated with books to read that make their review queues long. Remember that many free review sites have reviewers do this on their off time, and since they are not paid to review, they typically have a normal 9-5 job that only allows a certain amount of time to review books, so it may take a while.

NETGALLEY

Another great way to have your book reviewed is by joining NetGalley, which is a platform that hosts books and reviewers all on one platform. Reviewers from various media outlets as well as librarians, booksellers, educators, and bloggers use NetGalley to discover, read and share reviews about new books before they are published.

You do have to pay to have your book listed on NetGalley if you are an indie author (depending on whether or not the indie publisher has an agreement with NetGalley to hosts books) or a self-published author.

Keep in mind that although you are on the NetGalley platform, you are still one author amongst many waiting to get selected for a review. So even though you are paying for this service, there is a possibility that your book is not selected or reviewed prior to your release.

NetGalley can be a great tool, but you have to determine whether it is right for you. It has been my experience with many authors that they want reviews right away, and this is definitely not where you will attain those reviews with a quick turnaround time. But it is a great platform to showcase your book, and if you are willing to be patient, it can be very useful for reviews.

Once you have a few pre-publication reviews in place, you are ready to delve into your public relations adventure.

CHAPTER 7:
FINDING YOUR TARGET AUDIENCE AND NICHE

I can't tell you how many times I have sat down for a consult with an author and asked them who they would like me to reach out to only to receive a blank stare. So many authors don't know where their expertise and their book will fit in while the other half think it will fit in everywhere. The latter is typically wrong while the former needs to really figure it out.

Every book has a target and a niche audience. Some books may have more than one target and/or niche; also, more than one niche can be found within a target. The most successful campaigns I have ever worked on all involve the author and I finding various targets and niches to exploit at the right time. Finding something or a group that is very specific to target is much more effective than being general with your work. Don't worry about turning some people off and away from your work, because you are catering your outreach to a specific group or set of groups and subsets. I have found that through pitching to very specific niche outlets and audiences, other more general outlets and audiences will follow suit. But the best way to start is by finding whom your target and niche audience is.

A niche is always a part of your target audience, but a target audience isn't always a niche. Target audience and niche seem to get interchanged often, but your niche is a fraction of your target audience. Confused yet? Here is a closer look at the difference between the two.

TARGET AUDIENCE

According to Dictionary.com, your target audience is: *"The intended group for which something is performed or marketed;"*

To clarify, it is the specific group to which the messaging or content of your book is aimed at.

NICHE

According to *Dictionary of Creativity: Terms, Concepts, Theories & Findings in Creativity Research's* Editor Eugene Gorny, your niche audience is:

"Relatively small <u>audience</u> with specialized interests, tastes, and backgrounds. Many important forms of social creativity are of direct interest only to niche audiences."

These are the groups of people within your target audience who receive marketing messages in a **specific** and **specialized** context. These are the groups **in** the target audience that we weed out and connect with based on their behavioral habits.

Distinguishing the differences between the two can help propel your campaign by using pertinent information to create content specific to the needs of your target audience while placing it in the right context for the niche we are focused on.

Remember this as you build and create your PR campaign for your book.

How do you differentiate your niche and target audience for your book?

This may be really easy or a bit challenging depending on the content of your book and your expertise. If you wrote a book that is a "how to" for online dating then your target audience would be singles that use or want to use online dating platforms. Your niche, depending on how specific the content of your book is, could be baby boomers that need a bit more help with online dating. Another niche can be recent divorcees that want to start online dating. Is it starting to get a little clearer?

Authors and experts often lump everyone together based on the target audience without focusing on the best methods to reach each subset of consumer (niche), which can leave out some really great groups and possibilities. So take your time when identifying these groups for the best possible campaign outcome.

CHAPTER 8:
THE DIFFERENT TYPES OF MEDIA COVERAGE

So what type of coverage are you looking for? If you just said, "I dunno, just media coverage," then you need to understand a few key things.

Not all coverage is the same. If you think that coverage is coverage, then talk to some of the ad agencies that place their clients as experts for thousands of dollars versus placing a logo of a company. The cost difference is significant, because the effect it has on the consumer is significantly different.

Let me be the first to tell you that we live in a day and age where you now have to "pay to play" which basically means that to be featured in many magazines and websites or even radio and television, you have to pay an "advertorial fee." It sucks, I know, but if it's worth it to you, then you might want to really consider where you will get the most bang for your buck with the RIGHT audience.

That being said, there are still many great amazing and life-changing coverage opportunities for the right book and author, you just have to know how to sell yourself and book to the various outlets out there!

Coverage varies from outlet to outlet, but here are the types of coverage that I typically find that my authors have a better chance at:

For Print and Online Media
- Reviews of the Book
- Book Spotlight
- Author Spotlight
- Op-Ed/Opinion Piece
- Guest Articles
- Feature Articles

For Radio, Podcast, and Television
- Guest Interviewee about Book
- Guest on a Panel about a subject
- Expert

Let's take a deeper dive into each one of these so we can better understand what media outlets expect from each type of coverage category and what timelines you should plan for and expect to work with.

REVIEWS OF THE BOOK

These are pretty straightforward. It is usually an outlet via print or online agreeing to review your book and adding it to their review section for the day, week, or month. Depending on what type of outlet it is, it can take quite a while. Keep in mind that most staff at media outlets have been cut back, and there are less people there who are assigned to review books. This means that less staff/reviewers are reading more books. For this reason, before you reach out to these people know that you should give them, at least, three weeks to review the book. I generally approach them with a three month time lead prior to the launch of the book if I can, so that they not only have enough time to read and review the book, but it also gives me time to follow-up with them, and I am always taking into account their editorial calendars. Make sure that when you reach out to media during your follow-up that you are not feeling rushed or desperate for a review, which can (believe-it-or-not) come across in the email you send and definitely in the follow-up phone call.

When reaching out to magazines for reviews, always keep in mind that they all have an editorial calendar. Typically, for larger magazines, they are planning the coverage in their magazines at about four to six months out. This means that if you want to grace their pages, you need to know their editorial calendar timeline. We'll cover this topic more thoroughly in Chapter Eleven. So what does this mean for you? Well, it means that if you want be in the actual magazine, then you better start reaching out REALLY early, but if you are also good with gracing their website (which I tend to prefer), then you can keep the outreach at about a month and a half prior to your launch. I really like being a part of the online content, because you can always use that online mention on your social media to boost your clout and to boost your following. Also, you can ask the editor if they will add the links to your online platforms as part of their coverage, which they often do.

BOOK SPOTLIGHT

These tend to be the "easiest" and quickest to attain. It is usually a synopsis and a picture of the cover of the book along with a picture of the author in the media outlet. If it is online, you can add links to your book, website, and social media that link back and direct more traffic to your platforms. If your press release is great, the outlet might just regurgitate it onto their outlet. It's easy for them and great for you as long as you have a great press release. Book spotlights don't take much time for a media outlet to add to their content since they don't have to read the entire book and then write a review, you've pretty much already done the work for them. But you do need to make sure that the spotlight is timely or ties into their editorial calendar. What I mean by this is that if your book is older than a month or two, make sure that the content of your book ties into the theme of upcoming issues. You should pitch these at about one month prior to your book being published.

AUTHOR SPOTLIGHT

This is along the lines of the book spotlight except that they highlight you as an author and your expertise and **all** your writing and work. You can typically find these in Journals and Magazines as well as a lot of online literary and entertainment media sources. These are great to solidify your expertise and to direct media to your platform, which can later promote your book, or all your books for that matter. Typically, the timeline on these are not as long those of a book review and they tend to move in the same fashion of a book spotlight as far as timing and generally apply the same guidelines. These tend to work great for non-fiction writers. If you happen to be a Yoga expert and have written a book about some new and revolutionary type of Yoga or something of that nature, you can approach a Health and Wellness outlet to spotlight your expertise and your approach, but it doesn't have to necessarily be the book. This is a great way to have people look at you in not only a positive and expert light but also in a way to bring awareness to the approach which will, in turn, have people wondering about the book. Sometimes when you give people just a taste of your content like quotes from the book or information that only you know, it leaves them wanting even more which will bring them back to your platform.

Op-Ed/Opinion Piece

These are great opportunities for many authors, especially when it comes to fiction. Fiction writers tend to have a harder time getting media coverage outside of media that covers books, but a savvy fiction writer can use the research that they've used in their work to write about a current cultural hot-button or topic. An example of this would be a political thriller novelist writing about the current state of politics or something that ties into your book. Does Benghazi remind you of a situation in your book? Much fiction is rooted in truth, and if you did your research, then chances are that you have a big opinion on the subject and something to say. Why not say it where everyone can hear it? I've worked with a novelist who once wrote a piece about gun control for the New York Times. He was a writer of Westerns, but his research and a past experience led him to be able to write a wonderful piece. So, as a Sci-Fi novelist, can you write about NASA or some really cool technology that is being experimented with or constructed? You sure can, but make sure that you know your subject and that it is somewhat covered in your book. Are you a fiction writer in a town with little options for writing groups in the school system? Propose an op-ed to your local newspaper or town magazine about why your town needs better writing programs at school and how it will benefit the future generations of your town.

Most people are familiar with op-eds and opinion pieces, but for those who aren't then let me give you a rundown. This is a piece that expresses the opinions of the author usually not affiliated with the publication's editorial board. It is a piece that should be used to persuade the audience's opinions based on your research or familiarity with the topic at hand and writing. So not only is it your opinion, but it is grounded in current facts and stats. If written correctly, this has the potential to really propel your credentials while showcasing your writing style.

GUEST ARTICLES

These are my absolute favorite! But for some reason, they are not the favorite for many authors that I have worked with. I get it, an author likes to write their novels or books or what have you, but I go by the old adage that a writer simply writes. I'm not saying that it's simple, but I am saying that writing is what you do best, so this shouldn't be a problem. If you don't like to write for things other than your books or blog, then you are selling yourself short, but I understand, and you can skip to the next category, but if you want to reach a wider net of potential readers, then read on.

Guest articles allow authors to be a freelance writer for various outlets. Writing a guest article for an outlet has so many perks and is just plain fun. I have actually ghostwritten a few and really enjoyed it. Sometimes they are paid, but most of the time, they are unpaid, but you will reap the rewards in so many other ways.

Guest articles establish that you are a good writer for a very large audience. A well-written guest article has propelled many authors' careers and sales. It not only establishes your tone of writing but it also establishes you as a credible writer to other media outlets. In the dawn of the ease of self-publishing, it speaks volumes if you have credits to writing for reputable outlets. Writing guest articles for other outlets also allows you to tap into the talent at the outlet and really connect with these people, so that the next time you need their book editor to take a look at your book, you already have a connection there that will help get your book in front of them.

Typically you have to pitch the article or the topic of the article before sending the editor the whole article finished. But this is great because you have the option of pitching more than one idea without having to finish the entire article, which saves a lot of time.

You will have better luck placing guest articles with online outlets as well as small papers and small magazines. The reason behind this is that they are typically short staffed and there is always a ton to cover so it not only helps you, but it helps the outlet cover topics that their readers want to see but that they don't necessarily have the manpower to fulfill. Take advantage of this! If you wrote a book on BDSM (I've really worked on a book about this) and did the research, then pitch an article to an online singles magazine or an erotica site about why you think it's such a big seller. Start writing about topics that you are interested in, like, know about, and are trending or relevant to you and your book, and you will see that there are plenty of opportunities to get your writing featured.

FEATURE ARTICLES

Feature articles are articles in outlets that make you the featured story. These are probably one of the most difficult types of placements to achieve. It involves not only selling who you are and what you wrote, but also your latest achievements that make you worthy of someone taking the time to interview and write a story about you and these achievements. Do not get a feature article confused with an author spotlight. Feature articles dig way deeper whereas author spotlights tend to keep it strictly top line and use the information that you give them about yourself in you bio with maybe a bit more but not much more. Feature articles really interview you and talk about your contributions to a topic along with your work and why those are important to the outlet's audience.

Feature articles are usually longer than an author spotlight and also tend to tie in with the theme of the issue. So, if in an upcoming issue of Parents Magazine they are going to be highlighting issues parents of special need children face day to day then they might be interested in people who have made great contributions to advancing the discussion of special needs students and what they need in the school system. If you happen to be that person, you could possibly be the subject of that feature article.

Features are what everyone wants but most people don't fill the credentials for them. Just because you wrote a book doesn't mean that you deserve a feature in a magazine. Sorry, but it's true.

An old PR professor of mine back in college used to ask me all the time, "Who cares?" or "Why should I care?" I would have to come up with an answer that was both compelling and TRUE. If you can't come up with that, then chances are a feature might be a longshot.

BROADCAST

Broadcast is a great way to reach a vast and diverse audience. It is also little lighter and easier to work with when it comes to timing in comparison with other media avenues to take, but there are still some options and general guidelines that you should consider and keep in mind. Whether it is a national or regional news show, your book on air has the potential to reach a really wide audience. As mentioned earlier, there are a few key types of broadcast coverage. They are:

- Guest Interviewee about Book
- Guest on a Panel about a Subject
- Expert

Unlike print (especially magazines), you do not have to reach out to broadcast three months in advance. As a matter of fact, if there is some burning topic in the news going on right now and you happen to be an expert, then reach out right away! Strike while the iron is hot as they say. Although broadcast has a shorter lead time, please know that you must have not only done your homework when it comes to the outlet and what they have covered recently, but you must also have a solid foundation and experience as to what you are pitching them on. So what that means is that if you are pitching them to be an expert on their show about a topic that you think would be great for the show, you better actually be a legitimate expert! Be honest when you pitch your experience. Just because you might have had some experience with a topic does not make you an expert, but it can still make you a guest. Also, make sure that you have done your research on the outlet that you are reaching out to see how they have covered that topic in the past and explain to them how you can either enhance their coverage on that topic (if it is ongoing or will be covered again) or how you would be a great expert to have as a follow-up on that topic.

For example, if you recently saw a feature segment on a news show about veterans and Post-Traumatic Stress Disorder and you are a psychologist that specializes in working with veterans who have PTSD, then you might want to approach them as an expert on the subject for future segments on the topic if they revisit it. You might want to tell them how you would be the ideal expert for their audience based on your credentials and what you would cover that is different than what they already covered. You can also tell them how your expertise is revolutionary or more in-depth than what they already covered.

Another example would be if you recently saw a feature segment on a news show about veterans and PTSD and you are a dog trainer or part of a rescue group that trains dogs to be companions for those suffering from PTSD. You can pitch yourself or your rescue group as a follow-up to the first segment. Since the news show first featured those suffering from PTSD, a great follow-up to that segment would be groups or people helping to heal and cope with PTSD.

The bottom line is that although you should strike while the iron is hot, you should also do your homework and make sure that you are qualified enough to be considered an expert or a source.

I recommend that you start with local and regional and then move to national outlets, because most National Outlets will want to see that you have had some on camera experience before having you on.

GUEST INTERVIEWEE ABOUT BOOK

This is what ALL of the authors I work with want and ALWAYS ask me for, so I am pretty sure that this is something that you are striving for as well. This is typically what authors dream of: going on a national news show like TODAY, being interviewed about their book by Matt Lauer, and then having it take off in sales. Am I right? Well, if you are dreaming of this, then good for you, because you are dreaming big and you should!

You and your book have the power to affect and change the lives of so many people. It's all about being able to get it heard. And you can do this!

As a guest interviewee about your book, the staff at the news show will request the book and read it and then interview you based off of what they read. Keep in mind that they may not read the entire book, so you have to be on you're A-game for these types of segments. Depending on the media outlet, they might have the greatest interview for you, or it might be your duty to prepare your time on air in the direction that you want it to head.

If you do land a spot for a live interview (most of the news segments that I have worked on have been live), make sure that you ask the booking producer how long the segment will be. Having to plan for a 10-minute live spot on air is a lot different than planning a 3-minute spot (which tends to be a common recurring number for interviews that I have placed).

Now comes the planning for this. What are the KEY MESSAGES that you want to get across to the viewers and potential readers? Keep in mind that when live on air, time flies and if you aren't on your talk game, then your allotted time can pass by and you will realize that you didn't get one point across. There have been a few times this has happened to people that I know (even that I have worked with) who didn't care to get the right media training beforehand. ALWAYS PREP! This is a major rule of thumb. I have had some authors with whom I have tried to prep beforehand, and they were positive that they would do better if they just were to wing it. Turns out, they didn't wing it as well as they thought. In a three-minute interview, it is quite easy to just answer questions and not weave key messages into those answers. I have sat and watched interviews that were cringe-worthy and have been quite disappointed at a lost opportunity. These have ALWAYS been with an author who has refused to prep. Not only should you prep your information, but you should also have a friend or mentor help you with a timed "mock interview." I do these with my authors often and have them do a few exercises before the interview. For more on this topic, visit my website for some fun exercises to download for your next on air interview: www.DoGoodPRGroup.com/interview-exercise.

Typically there should be three things that come across your interview. Take a look at the following list:

1. Who you are and your expertise.
    Potential readers and viewers typically would like to know who you are and what gave you the authority to write this book. If it is fiction

and you are a local on a regional news show, tell them how the city from inspired your work. If the book is about a problem we face or could be facing, tell the viewers and host how you came to find this problem and how you are equipped to handle it. People need to form an emotional connection and trust in you, and the way to do that is to appeal to their emotional ties to the subject at hand. If you have an emotional story about how you became an expert in the subject or you went through something that got you to this point, then tell that story. But like in all public relations matters, tell it succinctly and make sure it fits in the timeline allotted.

2. Why the audience should read your book.
   This is the easiest for my authors to answer but also tends to be the most long-winded, because they try to appease the general masses. Don't do that. If your book has a special niche audience—which it will—then you should make your case to that audience, especially if they tend to be a general viewer; chances are they are the ones who are most likely to read your type of book to begin with, so why not direct them to yours?

3. Why your story is important/what you want the audience to take away from your story/book.
   This tends to be the hardest for my authors to answer. Most think that they are writing a book

just to entertain, but most influences of books are rooted in some deeper message of a factual event or situation whether you know it at first or not. As an artist/writer our artistic minds tend to be able to interpret and create a story based off of true-life events. Many times a fictional character is rooted in someone you wish to be, someone you know, or someone you have been or all of the above. Stories are created as a way of ourselves healing and exploring who those people really are and how we can control them. It is this that you need to explore before you find out why the story is important. What message or lesson will a reader pull from your story? Find that out and make sure that you let viewers/ listeners know what that message is. It could be just the message that people are looking for and need to hear.

The bottom line is that his tends to be most authors' dream coverage for their book, so use it wisely. Just because you may have landed this news segment easily doesn't mean that they are easy to come by. And even if they were, the best way to talk about your book is to prepare for it. So make sure to prep and to know these three key points. Once you have these dialed in and ready to express, it is easy to fill in longer periods of time by adding the details.

GUEST ON A PANEL ABOUT A SUBJECT

If you watch CNN or Fox News, I am sure that you are familiar with their news shows having different panels that consist of about six or so analysts about a topic. It can range from politics to law to healthcare to fashion and so on. Each one of those panelists is considered an expert of some sort in their respective field and topic of conversation. These types of opportunities are a great way to get involved in a conversation that might already be taking place. If you see that there is a hot button issue (that you are qualified to offer your expertise to) already driving discussions online via social media or forums, then chances are that so has a producer and ergo, it is a great idea to offer up your expertise and view on this topic.

Many times you will find that there are other experts that know a facet of the topic you cover more in-depth. You might also find that another expert knows about a topic that compliments yours or that can provide a good debate for your topic. If you happen to know of any that might make for a great discussion, suggest it to the producer that you are pitching (more on pitching later). If you can wrap up a nice package of a segment that is already a hot button, then you have a better chance at being a part of that segment. Keep in mind that this doesn't always directly promote your book, but it could. For instance, you are not going to directly talk about what your book is about by stating "in my book, I..." as it sounds like shameless self-promotion, and we don't want to come across that way, but what we can do is ask the producer to have the anchor or host of the show mention your book in your introduction, which they are generally always happy to do.

Before your date for this panel, make sure that you really do your homework on not only refreshing your insight about the topic but also on the viewpoints of the other people that will be on the panel with you. It is always nice to give someone accolades on the progress that they have made for a certain cause or their knowledge of a topic. This is a great way to gain not only colleagues that can help you in the long run, but also gain friendships that can be beneficial to you all. It is always great to keep likeminded or even opposite minded people close—so long as they provide an intelligent viewpoint that you can learn from and grow.

EXPERT

Being an expert on a show is a great way to solidify your credibility and platform. It is generally one of the best ways to up the ante of your game. As an expert on a news segment, you will be interviewed about a topic that your book covers, which the audience can then revert back to your book for more information. An expert on a show can help weigh in on current events and affairs that they are literal experts on. This means that you should have formalized training and be certified in some way to take action and talk about the situation.

Just saying that you are an expert when it comes to something (just because you have done it) will not fly. Please keep this in mind and make sure that you have factual and valuable content to provide an outlet before you begin to pitch an outlet about your expertise.

SUMMING IT UP

We've gone over quite a few different avenues that you can take when promoting you book during your PR campaign. These only have to do with media. I know that there are a lot and it might be a lot to take in at the moment. But after your head stops spinning consider this: there are a ton of ways for you to pitch and place your book and self. You just have to find the right one. Always keep in mind that the world and universe conspired and inspired you to write your book. You have an important story to share with people, so make sure that you do just that!

CHAPTER 9:
BUILDING YOUR TARGET MEDIA LIST

Now that you've found your target and niche audience and have an idea of what type of coverage you are going for, let's build a stellar media list!

First thing is first: what audience do you want to reach out to? What outlet do you want to see yourself and your book in?

If your answer is *Men's Health Magazine*, but your book is a Young Adult Science Fiction novel, then I would highly reconsider. Unless you have some amazing angle or spin to it, but chances are that won't be the right fit.

If you have no clue where to start or where you think it should be featured, do a bit of research on titles that are similar to yours or authors that have similar writing styles. Take a look to see who has covered and enjoyed their books and note them on your list. If you share the same type of experience or expertise with someone notable, take a look to see where they have been featured and add those outlets to your list.

If during your search and list making process you find that the list of outlets does not include the name of the person of whom you should or want to reach out to, then this is where your research skills are going to come into play. It is always better to address your email to a person, or if not an individual, then a department.

For magazines and print and online outlets, you will probably have the best luck looking for a book reviews editor if you are going for a review or author spotlight. If you are going for a feature for something that your expertise can highlight, then send that pitch to the features editor. Larger outlets have varying types of features editors, whose names can be typically found on their websites or in their issues. If you can't seem to find them, a simple Google search might reveal that they have their own website, because they like to create their own content on their own time aside from editorial calendars. If you reach out to them via their website, I have found that many find it flattering that you took the time to research their writing outside of their workplace.

If the person you are trying to reach is on social media, then you can send it that way, but be warned that some media contacts do not like this form of pitching. But if you were to engage in a Twitter conversation with them that they were already having or strike one up that pertains to what they have been talking about or reporting on, then it can be seen as you engaging with them and could be a great foot in the door. As part of many campaigns, my team and I always engage in Twitter conversations on behalf of our author, and it has turned up some really great results, but it has to be very organic and natural. Never force your ideas on someone on their public social media unless they have opened up that conversation already.

Bottom line, contacting someone through social media is okay. I have never had a problem with it but, like in all pitching, you have to do your homework.

CATEGORIZING YOUR LIST

You will find that it is much easier to build media lists based on categories. For instance, if you have a list that has many outlets, but in some you would make a great feature while in others it would be for a book review, make sure you separate those out into two separate lists. And from that, if you have some that are print outlets and others that are radio outlets, then separate those as well. In the end, you will have a total of four lists. If they are all arranged by category, it tends to be an easier and clearer way to keep track of all of your pitching lists.

I find that I can have about eight to ten different lists when breaking down one list. I tend to break down my lists like this:

Print/ Online Version of Print (newspapers—local to you or to your hometown/also can be local to where your book takes place)

Feature Editors
Book Review Editors
Business Editors (if the book is about business, etc.)
Online Editor

Online (blog/news)
Feature Editors
Book Review Editors
Entertainment Editor (if the book is written by someone famous or about someone famous)

Magazine (national/regional/local)
Types of magazine
Journals
Trade
Review
Lifestyle
Anything that pertains to the topic you are writing about

Broadcast
Television
News Regional
News National
Niche Specific Shows
Podcast
Segregated by Topic of Podcast
Radio
Regional or National (like NPR)

Although you are producing media lists for your book, you have to think wide enough to where it isn't only the book that you are making the lists for but also for you and the book topics. Keep this in mind always.

The more detailed and segregated the list, the better chances that you have of connecting.

CHAPTER 10:
GETTING YOUR PITCH READY

Your pitch is your number one way to sell your book. Have you thought of it yet? If someone asked you, "Why should I read your book?" What would you say back to them? Go ahead, practice. What if someone asked you, "What is your book about?" Can you answer that? I'm guessing that you can definitely convey what your book is about since you've spent so much time crafting it. And I can bet that you can give me many reasons as to why I should read your work, but how succinct is your answer? If your answer is longer than two minutes, then chances are that you will lose your audience. They are will already become uninterested, because you couldn't grab their attention quick enough. That's right: you have about two minutes to capture their attention before they check out.

I always have authors who tend to have an issue accepting this hard but true fact: in a world of social media, technology that gives you the information in a second, and thousands of competing media sellers vying for consumer attention, you need to send you message quickly and succinctly or you probably won't capture the attention of the consumer. The response that I get to this is typically, "Well, that's not the reader I want anyway." WRONG! You want **all readers** and if you say otherwise, you will never be a bestseller. Sure, you have to market to specific reader groups and target demographics, but at the end of the day, your ultimate goal is to get your book into the hands of just about everyone possible. And it is because of this that you have to NAIL down your pitch.

WHAT IS A PITCH?

A pitch is your presentation of what you are selling (your book and yourself as an author) whether it is by person-to-person communication or email communication to your prospective buyer—this can be either a professional reviewer or your average reader.

Basically you are soliciting them to read or review your book.

THE INFAMOUS "ELEVATOR PITCH" AND HOW TO APPLY IT TO PITCHING MEDIA

Chances are that you've heard someone at one time or another mention the infamous "Elevator Pitch". What is this staple in a seller's world? It is the one-two minute explanation as to why your book/you yourself as an author should not be dismissed.

If you were stuck in an elevator with a person for one-two minutes, how would you use that time to not only describe your book but also make them want to read it? How will you intrigue someone? What can you say that will capture their attention?

These things are what you have to know and have as a reference before you begin pitching to media outlets and readers formally for reviews.

Typically your elevator pitch should be about 25 words or less. Think of a soundbite. What would the soundbite of your book be? It should have not only the logline of your book, but it should have the emotion attached to it as well. When you sell your elevator pitch, you are selling yourself as an author because you are saying, "This is my work, this is how great it is, and this is why I am a great writer."

Once you know what your elevator pitch is you can begin crafting personalized pitches to each of your potential reviewers.

DOES ONE PITCH FIT ALL?

Nope. Not at all.

Remember when I told you that some publicists would use a one-size-fits-all approach to a public relations campaign and how it doesn't work? Well, the same applies to pitching.

The first thing that you need to ask yourself is: "Who do I want to read and review my book?"

Answers are different for everyone. Some authors want another highly revered author to review their work in the hopes that it might tap into their platform or maybe just for the honor of being reviewed by someone whom they admire. Some authors want reviews from media outlets so that it taps into their readers and gives them a reason to buy the book. Other authors want a television or radio producer to read the book to create the potential for them becoming a guest on that show to talk about their work. Whoever it is you want to review your book make sure that you know who they are, what their interests are, and what they like. You definitely don't want a bad review, but if you reach out to the wrong person you might just get that.

Make a list and ask yourself these questions:

- Who is my target audience/reviewer?
  Define who the perfect person for this book is and see how this person stacks up against your list of reviewers. You may find that you need to rethink your list or that perhaps your target reader can be a bit broader.
- Do I want a reviewer with a large following?
  It is always nice to tap into someone else's fan base and following especially if they are big influencers. But, depending on how they review

your book, this can either be very good or very
bad. Ask yourself if you are willing to risk this.

- Do I want quality or quantity?
  You can get 20 book bloggers with small
  followings to read and review your book at a
  nominal fee, which will boost your review
  scores on sites, such as Amazon and Goodreads.
  If this is what you are looking to do then you are
  going for quantity because the only leverage
  this will provide are ratings, but most likely,
  these won't get you on a talk show or any other
  bigger media outlet with a larger and influential
  fanbase to discuss your book.
- Do the people on my list like books like mine?
  One of the best ways to find a perfect reviewer
  for your book is to compare your book to one
  that's already been published (sort of like the "if
  you like this, then you'll like that"-way of
  thinking). Find books that are similar to yours,
  look at who has reviewed them, and then add
  them to your list.
- What is the current situation and timing?
  Is there something being talked about or
  something that has been buzzing that you can
  tie your pitch to? If you are a political expert,
  are there elections coming up? If you are a dog
  trainer, is National Dog Appreciation Day
  coming up? Are you a professional
  matchmaker? Well, maybe you can tie in your
  expertise into Valentine's Day.

- Keep in mind that many media outlets—
  especially what we consider "long lead" media
  (IE magazines and journals)—have editorial
  calendars that they maintain. Some of these are
  easily searchable through the Internet. This will
  tell you when their deadline is to receive
  pitches and material for future issues. We will
  cover this in the next chapter.

Research is key when it comes to reaching out to
reviewers for your book, especially those that will have
the most influence over potential readers.

REACHING OUT TO MEDIA

There is the reason I get paid to do what I do. It takes
time, dedication, more time, and a lot of well-timed
persistence. Not many people have the time and
patience to do this (not to mention the right training),
BUT if you do have the time and patience, then read the
following carefully for the training. Will you become a
PR professional after reading this? No, but you will
definitely have a better idea on what to do to promote
your book to the right people like a professional.

Reaching out to top media people can be very
intimidating. Heck, I do it every day and am still
intimidated—and that's a good thing. You want to be on
your top game when reaching out to these people who
can possibly be the game changers for your book, so the

number one rule is DO YOUR RESEARCH! Find out what they like. Follow their social media. Take note of what they've reported on that can be a springboard for your pitch. Keep in mind that you are reaching out to people who specialize in reading pitches; so make sure that your pitch is not only flawless but also tailored specifically to them and their outlet. Just because you change a few words or the name of the person whom you are pitching doesn't make the pitch tailored to your desired target. Know your target and reach out to them individually! It may be tempting to send a mass email via services like Mailchimp or Constant Contact, but do not do it! Show the people that you reach out to that you took the time to get to know their interests and are really sincere about thinking that they will like your book. People appreciate when you show that you really care what their interests are and aren't just shooting into the dark.

Looking to get booked on that popular regional news morning show? Well then, find the name of one of the segment producers. Watch your local news and see when they have other authors on air or human interest stories like cooking demos, pets for adoption, and other fun and quirky stories in the studio and take note. If you can offer something along those lines for your book, then look online for the name of that time period's segment producer or call the studio directly and ask. Many studios have more than one, so be prepared to gather as much information as possible.

THE PITCH FORMAT

As I mentioned earlier, if you are pitching editors and producers, you are pitching people who not only have to sift through hundreds of emails a day, but also have to do their jobs. For this reason, your pitch about your book has to be succinct and quick to read.

You can't expect someone who you don't have an established relationship with to take time out of their busy day to read a two-page letter of a pitch.

Your pitch should consist of the elements below:

1. A personalized greeting
    Make sure that you address it to the person that you are reaching out to and always, always, always remember to double check spelling of the name.
2. An introduction showing that you know what they like and you know what type of work they have covered in the past
    Nothing is better than first establishing that you already know what the reviewer or who the producer has worked with before. This shows that you are not mass emailing and that you really took the time to do your research.
3. A SHORT introduction about you and/or your work in the body of the email
    No more than three sentences. Whether it is of you or the book varies from book to book/topic

to topic. For someone who writes a non-fiction book about a subject that they are an expert on then chances are that it is probably a better idea to write about their expertise and accolades to show that they are a key expert in this topic. If the book is a novel, then chances are you should write about the book.

4. Follow the introduction with a sentence or two about how this pertains to their audience
Make sure that you let the recipient know how your book or expertise can add value to them and their audience. If you happen to be pitching a morning talk show in Oklahoma, make sure to tell them that the novel is set in Oklahoma with local landmarks and settings that their viewers can relate to and get excited about.

5. Ask for what you want
Always ask for what it is you actually want and answer why it would behoove them to grant you this. Don't just leave it up to them to decide what to do with the information that you just send over.

6. Give a few sample ideas
If you are pitching a guest article or a news segment, add a bullet-pointed list that has a range of 3-5 ideas for segments or articles that you can write. Add a small paragraph under each idea with an explanation. Make sure that if there are staggering facts or statistics about your topic that you know that you point them

out here! Producers and editors love to see interesting factual information. And always make sure to add if it is timely and/or local for that extra push!

7. Signature

   Duh! This is a given... BUT make sure that in your signature you have links to your website, social media, and link to buy the book on hubs, such as Amazon, etc. Making sure that there are easy ways to connect with you or check out your work in its entirety is one of the best and easiest ways to make sure that a reporter or producer digs deeper; if your social media and online platform game is on point (and it should be by now), then you are good to go!

8. Boilerplate

   This is a PR term, but it is basically a branded paragraph of more information about the item you are promoting. You can use this idea to put a short synopsis of the book and/or a short bio of yourself below the entire email. I suggest doing this, but make sure that it is again succinct. It should be shorter than the synopsis on the cover of the book, and your bio should be around 3-4 sentences.

Remember, the shorter the better, and try to refrain from putting unnecessary information in the email. That means pictures and attachments. It might be tempting to put an image of the cover of your book into the email but don't. You might think that you have the greatest cover design in the world and that it is a big selling point for your book, but chances are that it isn't going to make that much of an impact. What will to make the most impact are your words.

On rare occasion, it might be acceptable to add a picture of your cover. Note that I wrote *your cover*. Not yourself or a logo, some emoji, or ridiculous illustration in your signature or anything else for that matter—just the cover. On the rare occasion that this is acceptable, you should put it either below or next to your signature and it should be small.

Take a look at some sample pitches on our website (www.DoGoodPRGroup.com/pitching) for inspiration, and reference the sample pitches for what is acceptable when it comes to images.

YOUR SUBJECT LINE FOR EMAILS

This is something that I struggle with every day. The subject line of your email is what makes or breaks your outreach. It is the reason editors, reporters, and producers delete emails without even opening them, and is the deciding factor of whether your email is worthy enough of their time. So IT BETTER BE GREAT!

Subject lines are so complex because you only have a few characters to make it appealing and NOT sound like spam. In fact, there are email software programs that filter out emails if they have a subject line that sounds too much like spam. If this is the case, then it goes straight to the spam/junk mail folder, which tends not to be cleaned out often so your email just gets lost and wasted.

If you are proficient at using Twitter, then the skill that you have acquired of using 140 characters or less will definitely come in handy. Your subject line should tell the recipient what you want/have and why it's great in less than 140 characters. It should sell your idea without sounding *salesy*.

I recommend that you come up with three different subject lines for the same email. Once you have your subject lines, let them marinate on a Word document and come back to them in a while. Give them some time to settle and then, send three different emails to yourself with those subject lines to see how they look in someone's mailbox. Does part of it get cutoff? If that's the case, then rethink your subject line, so that all the MOST important information is showing in the mailbox or rethink the length of it. Then look to see which is more appealing and which you would open.

SLEEP ON IT

I know that you might be eager to send your pitch off once this is all set, but I highly recommend stepping away from your computer and coming back to this, not just in a few hours, but the next day. The old adage to "sleep on it" really makes sense here. You need a full day of pulling yourself away from the matter at hand to really clear your mind of it. Mostly so that you can catch mistakes and make edits. If you only give yourself a few minutes or even a few hours away from the material, the content is still fresh in your mind, and you will tend to read it the way you think it sounds. What I mean by this is that you are more likely to miss any mistakes that you've made, because the content is still on your mind. If you look at it with fresh eyes and a cleared mind, then chances are that you will find those small mistakes. And attention to detail is key. Your email might even sound a lot different than you thought it did the day before and now, you might have a better way to structure it. For this reason, you should plan to take two days to craft the perfect pitch and subject line. One day should always be for crafting while the second day should be for editing and giving it those final touches. Make sure you plan for this. There are exceptions from time to time like hypothetically, there might happen to be a breaking story or event that you just might be able to offer your expertise and knowledge to. If such a happening should occur then, by all means, craft your pitch the same day and send it off right away—time is of the essence. But before you do this type of sending off of a pitch, make sure that you already have a pitch crafted. What I mean by this is that pitches like these should not be the first pitch that you draft and send off. You should already have a few pitches drafted, and you can pull from those when in a hurry for breaking news.

I know what you are thinking—it's too much time to draft a unique pitch for every single person that you want to reach out to. This may take a lot of time, but I promise that it will yield the best results. You can either waste time by sending the same pitch to different people, or you can spend time that is worthy of your end goal. Great opportunities seldom come easily.

It is ok to use the frame of your pitch for more than one person. I mean, come on, how much can it really change? But the most important thing that will change from pitch to pitch is your research on the media contact and the value of you and your book to their audience/outlet. This is the reference to the person's work and why their audience needs to hear your story or why you would make a great guest on their show/why they should review your book. This can never be the same for two outlets, because each outlet is different and although they may provide close to the same content, the reference to their past work or why they should have you and your work will always be different. So although your pitch is different from person to person, it doesn't have to vary greatly, because you might be reaching out to similar outlets if they all are good fits for your book. Just make sure you are not taking the one-size-fits-all approach, because it rarely does.

CHAPTER 11:
EDITORIAL CALENDARS
& TIMELINES

If you remember from previous chapters I talked about how timing is everything. This seems to be true about many things in life, but it is definitely a prime factor of getting coverage for your book.

Media is always looking for NEW news. Remember that. This is why I always tell people to start building their platform as an author BEFORE you begin pitching your book to media outlets. Have everything to go months in advance before your publishing date. This seems to be the biggest problem for authors, and I totally get it. You have spent a long time writing and perfecting your novel or book; now that it's edited and ready to go, you just want to get it published. Well, while you are waiting on the publishing house to release it, if you are going the traditional publishing route, make sure that all your ducks are in a row like your media lists and knowing your editorial calendars. Make sure you have done all the research that you can beforehand.

Conversely, if you are going to self-publish your book, then the timing is all up to you, and you can plan accordingly, which is GREAT! Being able to control the timing of your book release is one of the best things about self-publishing, ESPECIALLY if you are putting a stellar PR plan into action.

So let's figure out how to make editorial calendars work for you!

The term editorial calendar means a calendar of the planned themes, features, and needs for upcoming issues of a magazine or other print and online media outlets.

Editorial calendars are made in advance as a way to keep a timeline and schedule going for the media outlet. They are often made available for advertisers, so that the advertiser knows who the ads will be targeted to, which is based on the content of the issue that the editorial calendar lays out. Editorial calendars are sometimes made public on an outlet's website. You can look for an editorial calendar on your targeted publication's website by either searching the writer's submissions page or contact page. If this doesn't turn anything up, you can look at the pages targeted toward advertisers or even call or contact the outlet's general email address asking for the editorial calendar.

Once you receive some editorial calendars, it will give you a general outline of what each outlet is looking for during the coming six months to year—yes, many outlets plan that far in advance!

Having the editorial calendar will give you an outline for future coverage, which will allow you to chart your pitch calendar as well. You can now begin to brainstorm how you will pitch yourself and your book to each outlet based off of their upcoming issues, timelines, and deadlines that they have set forth.

CHAPTER 12:
WAITING, RESPONDING AND
FOLLOWING UP

So you've followed my guidelines: built an amazing platform, got some pre-publication reviews, identified your target and niche markets, developed a calendar for pitching, wrote some stellar pitches, and finally sent them all off, so now what?

You wait. Yep, it's definitely a waiting game, and it SUCKS! I know, because I do this with almost every client! I also happen to be the most impatient person in the world (just ask my husband), but we literally have to wait it out—to a degree.

I typically wait a few days. Normally, I wait about four-to-five days before I send a follow-up email just to be sure that they received the first email. Many times if you have a signature in your email that has an image in it, the email will be flagged by spam filters and send to spam. This is another reason why it's so important to take those things out of your signature. Also, keep in mind that SO MANY PEOPLE RARELY CHECK THEIR SPAM

FOLDERS, especially if it is connected to an outside server like Google. Believe me, I know not just because I have had reporters and editors tell me they never received my email only to later find it in a pile of spam, but I also get email sent to spam all day. Also, they get sent to an outside server, so I literally have to log onto that server before I can take a look at my spam.

If that is the case, then send a SHORT one-to-two paragraph email asking the editor or producer if they received the last email you sent. Give them a bit of a rundown of what it was about and make sure that the subject line is compelling like the one in the first pitch.

Let me tell you that I have waited months before I heard back from someone. But persistence is the key to getting what you want. And let me just mention that there is a very fine line between persistence and harassment, and we always walk that line. For me, it has become an art, but it is constantly being refined. I once followed up with someone seven times before I heard anything back from them. But when I did they agreed to review the book. Now, I don't do that with every editor or media outlet, because that would be time consuming and a waste. But if I think that the book is a perfect fit for the outlet or for the editor or reporter to cover based on their track record, and if I am racking my brain as to why they haven't responded, then I keep on pursuing that outlet until they give me a hard-NO. And like I mentioned earlier, sometimes just getting that hard-no takes persistence.

CALLING AN OUTLET OR EDITOR

Do I ever call? Yes, I do, but that's because I have already established connections with certain media outlets. I try not to cold call, but sometimes, I have to. As a trained Public Relations professional, it is expected, but I do not suggest it for authors to do themselves. Let me explain why.

Being trained in PR, I am able to disconnect myself from the book and reach out to someone with quick and concise details that I think the reporter or editor needs. As the author of a book, you will not be able to do that. Believe me when I say that you will take tones of voices, curtness, shortness, and other things VERY personally. I don't take it personally because it's not my personal work. But you definitely will. And I know that even if you think you can separate yourself enough from your work, it is hard to do. Your book is like your child. You created it. You breathed life into it, and it's wonderful. But if you catch the wrong editor or producer at the wrong time, they can make you feel like it isn't worth their time and that can make anyone feel bad, and I never want you to undergo such unhappiness for wanting to share your work. So again, I say, don't do it. It is a lot harder to be rude via email, and although it definitely can be done, chances are you aren't catching someone off guard in an email and you can definitely catch someone off guard via a phone call.

GETTING A "NO"

If you ever do call an editor and don't get the response that you were hoping for, whatever you do, DO NOT ARGUE WITH THEM! Now I don't mean arguing like smack talking, because they don't want to cover your work. I am pretty sure that you know that this is completely out of the question. What I mean is trying to convince the editor once they are on the phone as to why they should cover your work IF they have already said no. I have seen this happen from time to time at trade shows where authors confront editors who didn't want to review their work, and it is never a pretty sight.

It's one thing to try and convince them via pitch letters, but if someone has already declined, then you shouldn't argue the fact that they don't think it's the right fit at the time. This goes for emails as well. This is not being persistent; it's being desperate. And if you act desperate, then you will definitely not make an impression that makes an editor want to read your book.

Always be gracious. If you get a decline via email or phone, thank them politely for their time, and if you care to ask them why they didn't think it was a good fit at the moment, then go ahead and do it but always be gracious.

If I feel that the editor would be receptive to that question, I always ask. It helps you to know for future pitching, and it may be that you need to change up your pitch.

WHEN THE RESPONSE IS A YES

So by now, you've either heard crickets, gotten a few no's, and a few I'll-get-back-to-you's. Then you get that amazing YES! "Yes, we want it," they write. "Send over a copy for review," they say. Now what?

Send it on over! Make sure that you also include a "one-sheet" of you and the book, which in the industry is literally a one-sheet (one document) synopsis of the book with the meta-data and the author bio. I like to add a little color and dimension to my one-sheets, because they can get a little boring. I try to make mine as visually appealing as possible since this is the one time that you can be as artistic as you please.

Send the sheet with as many books as they ask for via United States Postal Service (this is how I typically mail books, because it is the most cost effective) as well as a confirmation email, letting them know when you sent it. I also make a note of when I sent the books and email in an Excel spreadsheet to have an idea of when to follow up.

After about a week, when you do follow-up with them to see if they received the book, ask them when you should expect a review. Typically, it takes a while, but in order to not bother them continuously, just let them know that you would like to know, so that you can note when to expect it so that you may plan to add it to your social media channels.

Once they give you an estimated date, mark it on your calendar/Excel spreadsheet, and then, feel free to check back in at around that date.

RESPONSES TO PITCHES OTHER THAN REVIEWS

If you've pitched a guest article based on an idea, make sure that you can have a finished draft to them before the end of the week that they accepted it or by their deadline. Not having something to an editor by their deadline is completely disrespectful and shows that you don't value their time or the outlet. If you can't have the article done and in top shape by their deadline then don't pitch it. If you have pitched and the deadline is just completely not doable, then ask if they can have an extension. Don't wait until the last minute to ask, ask for the additional time beforehand. Doing so at the beginning will help let the editor know so that they can fill in or replace the space that they planned on using for your article.

If you get any of your pitches for guest articles, features or interviews are rejected, then ask if there might be a better time to re-pitch your topic. It might be that it just doesn't fit into their issue at the time, but if they need you in the future, then it's always nice to keep that door open. Let people know that you are always available, because putting yourself out there will definitely open up doors for you.

PROMOTING YOUR COVERAGE

Just because media outlets are covering your work or you and your expertise, it doesn't mean that you should solely rely on that for promotion. You should always use the coverage and capitalize on it by adding it to your online platforms and social media as well as your media kit. Always maintain your coverage on your "media page" on your website as it acts like your references to you résumé and shows all the different ways that you or your book(s) have been covered and the different mediums that you are able to present your work on. This helps to garner even more coverage.

If you get some really nice coverage that has some great quotes that you can pull out and highlight, make sure that you add those to any follow-up pitches for other outlets so they can see what others are saying about you and your work. It might just convince whomever it is that you are pitching that they should review your work. Again, it's all about building credibility for not just your work but yourself.

SUMMING IT UP

Following up and responding to media may be intimidating at first, but as long as you take into account their time and always err on the side of politeness, it should be just as easy as responding to or answering emails from others. Always know that an editor or producer is on a timeline and make sure to ask what that timeline is so that you can best help facilitate your coverage and show the producer or editor that their time is valuable to you.

CHAPTER 13:
PRESS RELEASES, ONE-SHEETS, MEDIA KITS, AND OTHER MEDIA MATERIALS NEEDED

Although your pitch is probably the most important piece of your campaign puzzle, there are many other forms of media material that you will need. Different media wants different things, so make sure that you have them all on hand before you reach out. Some of the media materials that I always prepare beforehand by having a template for each are press releases, one-sheets, media kits, and event fliers as well as the various pitches.

In this chapter, we will go over each of these and discuss format and content.

THE PRESS RELEASE

The press release has been long used by many PR professionals to disseminate information about the product that they are promoting to the masses of the media. As a PR professional, I have used these for sending information to the masses regarding books. You can send a press release via a wire or you can email these to various news outlets. As much as a press release is an important element to your campaign and material, it isn't as vital as the pitch. I know many PR professionals who use the press release as their main form of reaching out to media, and I have found that this tends to not be the ideal way to connect with media. Although it is great to announce the launch of your book or a great event that is coming up, you cannot expect it to stand alone and garner large amounts of media attention or coverage.

I always use a press release as a prelude to a pitch IF I use one in a campaign. Again, I believe in pitching each outlet individually so that you really connect to whom you are pitching and make sure to do the research that is needed.

But if you are going to send a mass release then I suggest taking a look at the link on my website (www.DoGoodPRGroup/pressreleases), so that you can make sure that it is formatted correctly.

ONE-SHEETS

Earlier, we went over the one-sheet briefly when discussing shipping books to media once requested, but just to touch on it again, let's make sure that we know what elements we should have.

A one-sheet should have all the important elements of you and the book on (yes, you guessed it) one sheet.

It is a page long and includes the summary of the book, a bit about the author, all the book information, and your contact information. I typically design these using text boxes so that the one-sheet isn't flat and has a few visual elements to it rather than it look like a long letter. You also have to get a bit creative to be able to encompass all of the information in clear sections on the one-sheet. Remember, everything that we do has to appeal not only through your writing but visually as well. For some examples visit my website and take a look at some of my past author's one-sheets on www.DoGoodPRGroup/onesheets.

THE MEDIA KIT

One of the most important things that you will find that you need is a media kit, which is a comprehensive kit that has the essential and more in-depth information about your book, yourself, and sometimes your publisher. It is everything that you want to put in your pitch, but can't due to space restrictions.

Media kits are digital and/or print packets several pages in content that provide the reader with an overall sense of the book with more in-depth descriptions of characters and a thorough history of the author to highlight any great achievements or awards as well as give a more personal sense of the author.

I like to give media kits to book clubs, media contacts, producers, places where you've proposed speaking, etc.

Think of your media kit as your condensed version of your website. It includes all your notable information to "wow" the reader and also lets them know what else you are capable of rather than a pitch which focuses strictly on why they should have you as an interviewee, guest writer or speaker.

You don't necessarily have to wait for them to ask for the media kit either. Once they have expressed interest, let them know that you are attaching the media kit to the email for more information about the book and yourself. If they see something that intrigues and blows them away, then chances are that will produce more interest. But they have to make that initial contact, because no one likes getting attachments from email senders that they don't know. If and when they have responded to you, send it on over!

Each media kit should have a few parts to it:

1. The Cover
2. The Longer Synopsis
3. The Author Bio
4. Author Q&A
5. Book Information and Meta Data
6. Optional-Information About the Publisher

Let's go into each part a little more in-depth.

THE COVER

Remember when you wanted to get all creative and flashy with your pitch email to that media outlet and/or producer or editor? Well, now's the time to do it. If anyone asks for your media kit make sure that you have something awesome to show them! The cover is what invites them to keep reading. It's what grabs their attention; so make it visual and eye-catching. It's the same idea that applies to your book cover, which is why you want to make sure it looks great and makes people want to read more. Typically the covers of the media kits that I design have the cover of the book with my contact information since I am the one that most media connections will touch base with, but if you are the primary media contact, then put all of your contact information.

THE LONGER SYNOPSIS

The next page of your media kit should be the synopsis of the book, but it should be a longer version of it than in your pitch. In this version of the synopsis, you can add more flavor to those meat and potatoes. In the pitch, we aim for a synopsis that is concise and only contains information about the real meat of the book. In the media kit, we like to spice it up as much as we can. We can explain the characters a bit more or the setting more to make it more relatable and intriguing to the person who you will be sending the media kit to. If you want to add a few elements to the synopsis that highlight some of your characters or if you have a non-fiction book, you can add some really interesting highlighted facts or information that you want to make sure that you get across from the book.

THE AUTHOR BIO

Typically, the author bio in a media kit contains just about all the accolades that you want to make known to media so that they are able to highlight it during their interview or coverage. I tend to write bios for media kits a little different than I write bios for a website. While a website bio is hefty, you can choose to write it in any form you please. With a media kit, I tend to write the bio with the most important or media-worthy information up top. Kind of how one would write a news story. The top is all the most newsworthy information and the bottom, while it is still information that the media can use, is also the information that you don't care if they leave out.

Your bio can also be fun and quirky. If the tone of your book is on the lighter side, then your bio should echo that. Essentially your bio should really personalize who you are for the media, who should then be able to gauge in what direction they should steer their interview with you. So just remember that if you want to keep it light and fun, make sure that your bio doesn't come off as stuffy and pretentious. And as always, remember to add all your website information as well as your social media information at the end of your bio.

AUTHOR Q&A

Many media kits that I have seen don't contain an author Q&A in them, but I have made sure that the ones that I produce do. I find that having a Q&A in the media kit is helpful to guide media discussions of the book and author. It provides them with a special set of questions that they already know that you are prepared for and can discuss. I like including this, because it is sometimes what interviewers revert to if the media outlet doesn't have enough time to prep, and it makes sure that your message gets across; your Q&A in your media kit always includes the messaging that is important to you as well as what you want to get across to the reader.

The Q&A is a full page of getting your point across about the book. Sometimes book clubs or groups can use these Q&As to discuss the book as well. You can also add questions that you want the readers to ask themselves as they are reading the book. Here are a few Q&A questions that I typically add to media kits:

1. What inspired you to write the book?
2. What message do you hope readers take away from the book?
3. Why is this book important to today's readers?

You can get more specific based on your content but you get the picture, right?

BOOK INFORMATION AND META DATA

Providing all the right book information in your media kit helps with all the little details that we tend to overlook when thinking of overall coverage and sales. But at the end of the day, we are doing all of this outreach and campaigning to sell your book, so it is in your best interest to add information to your media kit that will help facilitate this.

I like to dedicate a full page to all of this information. It can range from simple things like the ISBN number, the name of the publisher, number of pages, formats that it is available, and all the links to the stores where you can buy the book to keywords for the metadata of the book.

Metadata is all the information used to sell your book and boost your rankings online with increased SEO. Now, media outlets will use not all the information on this sheet, but it is best to have any information in your media kit that will potentially help sell your books. Media kits are not only for media; sometimes you can send over a media kit to a book buyer to entice them to carry your book if you are doing any sales on your own. For any interested party, having this metadata will make carrying your book a lot easier since you pretty much did all of the work for them, especially when it comes to setting up metadata to sell the book. Having the metadata for the book is important for a few other reasons when it comes to media. For example, if the outlet that is receiving the media kit is a print media outlet with an online platform or if it is strictly an online media outlet, then they are able to use and may add some of the information from the metadata page that you have provided for the backend of your coverage: this means that your book and/or you will get increased search rankings as long as you provide all the right metadata.

OPTIONAL- INFORMATION ABOUT THE PUBLISHER

I like to dedicate a page to the publisher's information for many indie authors and authors who have started their own imprint. It is my strong belief that indie publishers are going through a great renaissance. Many indies are carrying a lot more clout than ever before. Some indies put out books that move on to become NYT bestsellers, and I think that many of these indies that are producing these award-winning and bestselling books fly under the radar for a long time before anyone gives them a nod. If an indie publisher publishes you, then it is your job as their author to always give them this nod if you feel that it is warranted—and if you signed with them, then you I hope that you truly do feel that way. Let the media know what their past books are if they are bestselling or award-winning. Share the quality of books that they have produced, so that others can see their great work and note that you are part of that. Showing that your indie publisher has a great track record not only helps to increase your credibility, but also the credibility of the book.

If you are published by one of the Big Five publishers, you may add information about the publisher, but there is less of a need as the names speak for themselves and are recognizable. If it is an imprint of a Big Five publisher and the name isn't as recognizable, then I suggest adding information about the imprint to make clear as to who the publishing house is.

If you are self-published and only plan on publishing this one book, then I would not mention anything about your publisher, because it is probably Create Space or some other self-publishing medium that isn't of interest to media outlets. To be honest, media outlets tend to shy away from self-published books, which is why I don't like to direct any attention to the publisher when I work with self-published authors. I am honest about it, but I don't highlight it due to the stigma that many people in the media associate with self-published books. But, if you are a self-published author and have built a publishing imprint with plans to publish more books (and have already set up that platform), then I suggest adding information about your publishing house on this page. You don't have to state that this is YOUR publishing house, but rather the mission statement of the publishing house, which you should already have in mind. There is nothing wrong with building in some PR for your publishing house if you truly plan on publishing at least 3 more books under that imprint.

With all this being said, this page with the publisher's information is not CRUCIAL, but it can be a good idea depending on who your publisher is.

FLIERS AND OTHER MEDIA MATERIALS

Although you will probably want to have a few different fliers—one for each event, it's a great practice to have a template for each flier with all pertinent information. That way you can just copy and paste the main information like book title, author, short synopsis, short bio, etc. to another flier or perhaps to social media and online calendars and event postings. Always make sure that you make material like fliers and/or invitations for events, especially for your book launch. The more personalized you make the fliers and invitations, and the more you let people know how much it will mean to you if they go, the better the chances are that they will attend.

I have met many authors that didn't want to ask the people they knew to attend their events due to either being shy, not wanting to seem like they were desperate or bragging, et al. But I have to tell you that when you accomplish something as great as writing a book, many people are proud of you and feel honored that you want them there to celebrate that great accomplishment. Invite as many people as you can, because it isn't desperate or facetious—it's considerate and polite. Let your circle know how proud you are and how they've helped you along the way in this arduous journey of writing. Chances are they'll be more than happy to not only come and celebrate, but also to spread the word about your amazing achievement.

CHAPTER 14:
THE BOOK TOUR

A successful PR campaign for an author doesn't just focus on media and reviews. It focuses on different ways to connect with your target reader and building credibility, which is why we reach out to the media in the first place. One of the best ways to reach out to that audience is to do a book tour.

Book tours do not necessarily have to be bookstore to bookstore. They can be at schools, at community centers, at different book groups, festivals, and on various panels. There are really many options for these, and it puts you in direct communication with your readers or people who are likely to be fans of your work or will look to you in the future for your expertise.

Limiting your book tour to only bookstores is not a good idea. Depending on what your book or expertise is about, there are a multitude of possibilities of where you can go.

Don't worry if you are in a small town with limited resources to travel and visit various groups or stores. Now with computer applications, such as Google Hangouts or Skype, you can have meetings and hold presentations around the world!

SETTING UP BOOKSTORE EVENTS

If you are planning on reaching out to bookstores to schedule events, there are a few key things that you should know. This is a great time for you to check to see if they carry or plan on carrying your book. Having an event at a store forces the bookstore to carry the book, because they know that copies will be sold during the event, so it is easy money for them.

If you were published with a traditional press, especially one of the top presses, then it is easier for the bookstore to order the books themselves through their distributor which is definitely what you want in order to be considered on bestseller lists. When bookstores order books via their distribution channels, your book sales get reported and recorded, so that they can one day be on that *New York Times* Bestseller List. The people who compile this list and many others get their data on book sales directly from bookstores and sellers as well as from Nielson BookScan. All rely on point of sale data from a number of major book sellers. When you are setting up bookstore events, make sure that the bookstore is one that reports their information to these lists.

It is always best to have the bookstore order the book on their end if possible. However, if they are not able to do so due to your book not being available through their distributor (this topic will be discussed in the next chapter), then you should definitely coordinate bringing or leaving your books at the store on consignment.

Typically consignment is when you agree through a written contract with the store to leave your books there for sale and split the profit once they are sold. Typically the split is 60-40 with 60 percent of the profit going to the author and 40 percent going to the bookstore. Although this is typical, it is not always the case and some bookstores might even charge you a shelving or placement fee. This means that you have to pay a fee to be on their shelves and unless your books are flying off the shelves, the fee and contract only requires the bookstore to carry the books for a set amount of time (usually about one-to-three months). Once the time is over, you either have to pay for shipping back to you or you can pick the books up if you are close to the store. If you have an event at the bookstore and the books sellout at the event, then they may ask you to leave more books and not charge you their normal fee. One of the main reasons that you should coordinate well-attended events at bookstores is so that you can sell books where they otherwise might not carry it. Just make sure that your events are well attended.

MAKING SURE THAT YOUR BOOKSTORE EVENT IS WELL-ATTENDED

So how do you have a well-attended event you ask? Well, there are many factors that go into planning a successful event; one is having a strong understanding as to whom your audience will be. Take into account the key factors of the book and of the store to know who it is that will be coming to the event.

If you think that just setting up an event at a store is all it takes, then don't be surprised when you get maybe a few people that show up.

Other considerations in setting up bookstore events are the following:

- Know Who Your Audience Will Be
- The Location of the Store
- Parking
- The Date and Time of the Event
- Planning/ Marketing Material
- Weather
- Time of Year
- Other Local Events

Let's discuss these in a bit more detail.

KNOW WHO YOUR AUDIENCE WILL BE

When you first start to reach out to bookstores for events, many will ask you right away who your audience will be and approximately how many people will attend.

This may seem like a hard question to answer, but it really isn't if you've done some mental planning. You are likely reaching out to a certain bookstore, because you know it and go to it often. It's probably near where you live or work, and it's most likely near family and friends as well. If you are reaching out to a local bookstore, then you already know who your audience will be. It will be friends, family, people from your writing group, co-workers, and so on, but if you are looking at a venue that is nowhere near anyone that you know, then you'd better have an idea of who your audience will be or else you will be reading to an empty room; if you can't tell the bookstore event manager who that audience will be, then you might not even get a chance to read at the bookstore that you want. If you can't guarantee a crowd, then a bookstore event coordinator typically equates that with no sales. So before you reach out, at least have an idea of your audience, and once the event is set, make sure you do all that you can to drive them there, because the bookstore will not.

Many authors that I work with think that once they have the event set that the bookstore will do the rest in driving traffic to the event. The bookstore won't. Even if it does mean more sales for them, it's not something that they generally do. The most they will do is hang some promotional material or leave fliers there, but driving traffic to your event is all up to you, so make sure that you reach out to local schools, local community centers, book clubs and writing groups, and anyone else that might benefit from the content of your book or your expertise.

THE LOCATION OF THE STORE

Some authors are really excited to get into just about any bookstore for an event, and why wouldn't you be? Bookstores are wonderful places that will help support your work. But location is a key factor to keep in mind when planning which bookstores you want to reach out to.

If you are perhaps planning on inviting all of your friends and family for your first event or book launch, but the store is really far out of everyone's way, then you should definitely reconsider. Try to find a bookstore that is close to the people that you plan on inviting; that way you have a better chance of people showing up.

Make sure that the store is also easily accessible. Is it close to a freeway off ramp or a train/subway station? Do people have to really go out of their way to get there? The easier it is to access, the better of a turnout you will get which always means more sales!

Another big factor is whether or not the location already gets a lot of foot traffic. Is it near cool restaurants or bars? What's the vibe like on the street that it's located on? If it's a ghost town around the store then there's a likelihood that there won't be people who randomly walk into the store for the event.

PARKING

This has recently become a factor for many events, and not just book events. Depending on where the bookstore is located, parking can be a major issue. I can tell you that being from Los Angeles, we can easily spend an hour searching for parking. When we don't plan accordingly, we might potentially miss half of the event that we planned on attending. On top of that, there are parking signs and regulations for EVERYTHING! Downtown Los Angeles and Santa Monica specifically are the worst when it comes to finding parking. So, depending on where you are from, this might play a factor on attendance and timeliness.

If parking is an issue where you plan on having your event, it won't be a problem as long as you let people know ahead of time on your promotional material or invites. For instance, you can say "limited metered street parking on X and Y streets—change only accepted in meters" or "parking structure behind bookstore at a rate of $10 for the entire night" or whatever else it may be. It gives people an idea of what to be prepared for. From there, they can plan accordingly, which makes the night flow better.

THE DATE AND TIME OF THE EVENT

Many authors are always concerned about having their book launch party on the date that it was actually launched/published. It is very tempting to have it on the same day, but there isn't really a definite need for it. If you would like to have on that launch day, then that can dramatically alter the guests attending your event.

Most launches/book releases are on Tuesdays. It just happens to be an industry norm. So does this mean that the launch party should be on a Tuesday? Not necessarily. Some people like to do this, and bookstores love it since it drives people into their stores on an otherwise slow night, but it might not be feasible for people to make it if they have jobs that require them to work normal business hours and then have to sit in traffic or have a long way to travel for work. I am not saying that you shouldn't do it, but I am saying that you don't have to. If you have your event within the first two weeks of the release date, it can really help with getting on bestseller lists right off the bat, but if you don't care about that, then you can even think about having it during the first month of the release.

Still planning on having it during the traditional workweek? Then try to have it at a time that is reasonable enough in that it allows people travel time in traffic after work. Setting an event on a Tuesday at 5pm makes it really hard for people, and they might even ask why you chose that time, knowing that many people are barely leaving work at this time. It shows that you are expecting them to leave early and shows a disregard for their schedules. But if you schedule your event on a Tuesday at 6:30pm, it shows that you took into consideration the travel time for most of your attendees and that you care that they attend. Of course, you can't accommodate everyone, but making arrangements that attempt to work with other people's busy schedules will make it so that people will do their best to return the favor in accommodating you and your book release, etc.

Weekend events are better for most folks. Think about the times that you generally go out or the times that people with 9-5 jobs go out. Happy hours are frequented most on Thursdays and Fridays, because there tends to be less of a workload at the end of the week. I have had great events on these days since more people seem to be in the mind frame of going out. Pair that with some free wine and snacks, and it tends to be a great time for unwinding after work with intelligent conversation and a mini/free happy hour of sorts.

Saturday and Sunday are all right as well. Just keep in mind that these are sometimes the only days that people can get things done. And if you plan something close to a holiday, chances are that people are using the weekends as extra travel days.

PLANNING/ MARKETING MATERIAL

Don't ever expect to have a last minute event go off great. There is a possibility that it can, but the probability is that it won't. In order to have great events, you must plan them one month to two weeks out. If you want to be in event calendars, then I would plan about one month out since some of the bigger event calendars need that much of a lead time.

There are many event calendars that you can submit your event to. For example, if you live in Los Angeles like I do, you can submit it to the Los Angeles Times event calendar. You can also submit it to Eventful, Yelp, The Patch, Zevents, and many other calendars. Submitting to calendars helps get the word out and also helps you spread the word via social media because you can share the event that you created in the event calendar.

Always make sure that you also create marketing material for your events: fliers, invites, and the like with all the pertinent information for the event, including the time, address, parking situation, duration, information about tickets and pricing, and if refreshments are being served. Make the flier fun and also make sure that you have a digital version, which you can attach to email and also upload it to all of your social media. Having a digital version of the invitation or flier is sometimes better, because you can embed links to the flier that allow people to get directions or allow people to RSVP to the event which can help with planning even more.

Reach out to local groups that might be interested in attending your event to let them know about it. This can range from book clubs, community organizations, college classes and writing clubs, etc. Make sure to offer them and their members something worthwhile for coming. You can offer incentives like the first two members of the organization who come and introduce themselves to you get a free, signed copy of your book. Or if you are charging for the event, those who are members of the group can get free entry. Many times, I have found that creative writing teachers at high schools and colleges are more than willing to offer extra credit to their students who attend bookstore readings and events because they want their students to be immersed in literary culture. So get creative, and think of who might benefit from your event.

WEATHER

I'm lucky enough to live where the weather doesn't change very much. California has the most temperate climate, which is why the weather rarely plays an issue in having events, especially if the events are indoors. But our climate can be a double-edged sword, because no one likes to go outside if it happens to rain a bit . In any case, weather plays an important role on an event, particularly if the reading is outdoors. An outdoor reading is great on a warm summer night with a wonderful glass of wine or cup of coffee. I have been to a few bookstores that have great outdoor reading series, but once in a while, no one goes if the weather isn't just right.

The weather typically comes more into play in places with snow and extreme temperatures. That's when you really have to be mindful of when people are willing to travel for events, such as book readings. If you do decide to have your event on a date when the weather is not what you wanted it to be, then make sure that you spice up the reading to entice people to come out even more.

I know that weather is not in your control, but try as much as possible to keep the weather in mind for your events. If you know a certain time of year is snowy and rainy, then try to veer away from that time of year when planning your book release and events.

TIME OF YEAR

I once had an event during the Fourth of July weekend in a place where it's typically quiet and I will not do that at a bookstore ever again. The time of year when you decide to release your book and have events really plays a part in attendance and sales when it comes to having bookstore events. Keep in mind times of the year when people and families— especially if they are your target demographic—go out of town or if you live in a tourist destination, the time when people are in town. Unless the store you are planning your event at is in a city or town that is typically a destination for tourists, then it might be a good idea to postpone an event on the Fourth of July. For instance, if I planned my event at a bookstore in Santa Monica that was at the promenade during the week of Fourth of July it would have been a better turnout because there is more traffic in Santa Monica during that time since the weather is nice and people head to the beach for the fireworks. However planning an event in Santa Monica on the same day and time at a bookstore that is not near the beach and perhaps that is closer to the college then I am going to get a much lower turnout.

OTHER LOCAL EVENTS

Another consideration should be is if there are any major local events happening around the time of your event in a nearby radius. This can either help or hinder your event. Some events, if the times are right, can help by increasing foot traffic to the bookstore that you are at. Other events might pull your audience away or divert them. If there is an event with road closures nearby or streets closed off it can greatly deter your audience. Always remember to check local listings and event calendars so that you are up to speed on what will be going on around your event so that you can either use it to your advantage or plan around it.

NON-BOOKSTORE EVENTS

Many authors that I work with think that bookstore events are the be-all and end-all. They aren't. In fact, some of the best events that I have had were NOT in a bookstore.

I always suggest mixing up the types of events that you have for your book tour. They can range from events in bookstores, speaking events at universities and colleges, panels at workshops, expos or conventions, hosting your own workshop at venues and many, many more. The opportunities are endless if you really think about and plan in advance.

The issue that most authors have with planning events outside of bookstores is that many don't ask a bookstore that reports sales to bestseller lists to handle their sales at these events. You may and should, in fact, ask a bookstore to handle off site sales for an event so that your sales are reported to bestseller lists, especially if you are looking to land on them. As long as the store that handles your sales is a store that reports to these lists, then you will receive credit for the sales of the books at this event and with all your events and marketing and PR savvy, it could just land you on a national bestseller list. Many people have events solely for this purpose; if this isn't your main purpose, but you plan on having a book tour around the launch of your book, then you might as well make sure that you leave all possibilities open.

When thinking of non-bookstore events such as conferences and book festivals to add to your book tour, make sure that you plan months in advance. Many conferences have deadlines for speaker entries up to a year in advance, and some also ask for some sort of sponsorship, which typically means that there is a fee or they ask for product for giveaway.

FINAL THOUGHTS ON YOUR BOOK TOUR

While a book tour is a great way to boost sales right off the bat after your book launch, always ask yourself what the main purpose of the tour is before you start planning it. Don't just do it for the sake of doing it. Make sure that there is a solid reason behind what you are doing so that you can plan accordingly and head in the right direction. While there are many different avenues that you can take, make sure that all the issues that we just went over are taken into consideration and planned around as best as possible.

Once you've done everything that you possibly could have to plan and execute each event, make sure that you enjoy it and have someone there taking pictures of you interacting at each event with guests for social media posts and engagement. Have fun!

CHAPTER 15:
DISTRIBUTION OF YOUR BOOK

Although you book's distribution doesn't have a whole lot to do with your PR campaign, it does come into play as part of the campaign when it comes to events mainly. In our last chapter, we discussed events and having them at bookstores or other venues, and I mentioned that we would revisit the topic of distribution of your book. While I am not going to spend a lot of time on this topic, I will explain what I have learned about distribution and how it has played a role in the public relation campaigns that I have been a part of.

Depending on the type of distribution set up for your book, you can have many hurdles that you might have to find a way to jump over when it comes to events or getting your books into certain venues.

If a traditional publisher publishes you, you don't have to worry about this and can move on to the next chapter, but if you are self-published and use print on demand, then take note. If you are indie published and aren't privy on their distribution methods, then start asking. In fact, this should be one of the first question that you ask any type of publisher that has agreed to publish your book, because it can be an issue later on.

The main distributors in the United States that I have worked with are Baker & Taylor, Publishers Group West, and Ingram. Many authors get confused by the word distributor and think that it means bookseller—it doesn't. A book distributor is a company that promotes and sells books to retailers, such as bookstores and libraries. Distributors also usually warehouse the books as well as sell them to these retailers through a sales team and their book catalog that is distributed to these retailers that they already have an established sales history with. So you see, the distributor is the middleman that MOST booksellers use to acquire your book, and it is a great middleman to have.

Many self-published authors want to be able to be a part of these major distributors and their catalog title lists, but it isn't always possible. And even though print on demand makes it possible to be listed in their sales catalog with Ingram Spark, it is not the same as distribution through a traditional publishing house's distributor.

Here's why. Although you are in a database with these distributors, and retailers are technically able to buy your book through that database, it doesn't mean that they will. Traditional publishers make sure to market their books to retailers and have a sales team driving book sales, and not only to retailers but also to that retailer's consumer. This drives sales further for the retailer, which helps to persuade them to stock their shelves with the book. With most traditional publishing houses, retailers are able to order books and **return** those that don't sell. This way they don't risk as much money loss buying from traditional publishers as buying from print on demand authors.

You can still get your books into some bookstores through some really great programs that some bookstores have for indie authors, but keep this in mind when you "think" that you have distribution like any other book.

WHY DOES DISTRIBUTION MATTER IN THE WORLD OF PR?

It matters, because when you plan and execute events for your book launch and are concerned about hitting bestseller lists, you want to be able to sell your book through a bookstore that reports to bestseller lists, so that your book sales register. If you don't have the right distribution, then you won't be able to do this.

One way to get around this is to have your guests preorder the book with the store before the event, but doing that tends to get a bit murky. One of the only ways that bookstores sell self-published books is through preorder so that there is no chance of books not being sold and that the book store won't be stuck with it. You can however ask to broker deals with bookstores if you are having an event there where the store buys the books that you are estimating that you will sell at the event, and if they don't sell, you will buy them back. I have seen this done before but not very often.

If you don't care about those bestseller lists, then you can have the book at the store on consignment. Depending on what store you would like to have an event at, this may or may not be a possibility. Bookstores that are large chains are pretty strict when it comes to distribution and events and typically lean toward having events in which the author's book is returnable via their normal process. So please be aware of this if you are self-published and want to have your event at that large Barnes & Nobel that a famous bestselling author was just at.

Keep this in mind and don't get frustrated at a bookstore turning you down because of distribution issues. Move on to the next bookstore or venue and keep a positive outlook.

CHAPTER 16:
MEDIA TRAINING

Whenever I set up a live on-camera or on-air appearance for an author or for any client, I always recommend media prepping before they go to the studio. There are people who literally make a living training you to be a great on-camera person and wonderful speaker, but if you are doing your own PR campaign, you're probably doing your own on-air prepping, and that's ok. There are just a few key things that you should make sure that you do beforehand to ensure that you can look and sound great on air, that there is no lull, and that you don't' get a case of "radio silence" because of surprises. Here are a few items that we'll be going over:

- Ask the Producer or Reporter About the Segment
- Make Sure Your Send Over Your Media Kit
- Go Over Key Questions and Answers
- Talk About Your Synopsis

- Practice, Practice, Practice; Then Practice in Front of a Mirror
- Find the Right Outfit

All right! Let's take a look at each more carefully.

ASK THE PRODUCER OR REPORTER ABOUT THE SEGMENT

I have worked with clients that had previously garnered media attention on their own only to ruin a great opportunity, because when it came time to present their product or book on air, they were at a loss for words. They thought that they were prepared since it was their book and were used to talking about it so much that they figured that talking about it on air would be the exact same thing, but it turns out it's not. For some reason when you are in studio or even in front of a crowd, if you haven't practiced enough and aren't prepared, it won't go as planned.

I always ask producers or reporters what the segment will entail and to give me as much detail as possible. It sounds nitpicky, but it really helps in preparing. I ask if they have specific questions in mind that they will be asking during the interview, and I make sure to note them and practice conversing around those questions, but I also make sure that my clients are open and ready to the flow of the interview changing as it often does.

Some reporters might wing it when it comes to interviews or coverage of your book, this happens often and you have to be prepared and ready to accommodate that. I try to prepare my clients enough to be able to guide the interviewer in the direction that they want the interview to go in order to promote their book. It is very likely that if you sent over the media kit, then the reporter will typically work with the information provided in it. This leads us to our next section.

MAKE SURE YOUR SEND OVER YOUR MEDIA KIT

After I talk to every producer or reporter, I always make sure to send over the media kit and let them know it's for their reference for the interview. I send it even if I have sent it before. I do this to refresh the producer's memory about the media kit or if is the actual reporter/interviewer that I am sending it to, then I resend it because sometimes, the producers might forget to forward the information along to them. This is always a must, because if you make sure to add the right information that we previously discussed about media kits, then you will have a great Q&A already for them to work with. This really helps to guide the discussion and also helps in your preparation.

GO OVER KEY QUESTIONS AND ANSWERS

Always go over the Q&A in the media kit but not only that, make sure that you go over other possible questions as well. If the producer gives you the questions that will be asked during the interview, then that is great, but if not, then make sure that you go over all your key points of the book. What is it exactly that you want the viewer or listener to know about the book? Some of the following questions are good cues to build on: Why did you write the book? How does this book/main character connect with culture/a specific group today? Who needs to read this book? Fans of which popular author would enjoy this book?

Make sure that you can answer all of these questions and more in quick and witty ways that are entertaining. And always keep in mind how long the segment will be which is usually around three minutes long. So make sure that the answers to your questions aren't longwinded or full of pauses or filler words.

The reason for doing this is so that by the end of the time that you take to practice these Q&A's, you will have a clear idea of what it is you want viewers or listeners of the show to know about you and your book. The worst feeling is coming back from an interview wishing that you had said something or brought up the best part about your book. Make sure that while going over your Q&A, you go over all the things that you feel are important.

TALK ABOUT YOUR SYNOPSIS

Can you tell me about your synopsis in a way that doesn't just go over characters and plots, but rather in a way that I can relate to or that will pull at my emotions?

There are many different ways to talk about your synopsis, but many authors only know one way to do so; sometimes they don't even know that way either. If this is you, it's ok, as long as you are willing to keep doing your media training.

Your synopsis isn't just a summary of your book; it's so much more. It's a way to tell people why they should read it and who would enjoy it.

For example, this book that you are reading isn't just a book for authors that want to build their own PR campaign. It's a book for authors aspiring to be bestsellers and willing to do what it takes to make that happen with tried and innovative PR techniques that they can do themselves and have been proven to work to garner media attention without having to spend thousands of dollars on PR representation. See what I did there? It may be subtle, but it strikes an emotional interest in the book, because I painted a picture of who needs to pick up my book – a driven author who is willing to do what it takes to be a bestseller that doesn't have the budget for a traditional PR campaign. Use words that strike emotion or connection.

Once you have 2-3 different versions of your synopsis written down, then make sure to go over them often.

PRACTICE, PRACTICE, PRACTICE; THEN PRACTICE IN FRONT OF A MIRROR

It may seem trivial or you may feel dumb talking to yourself in front of a mirror, but you need to do it. I like doing this with my authors when they tell me that they don't need media training. I say, "Ok, then let's practice. Pretend I'm the interviewer." Then I ask them, "So Mr. X, tell me about your book."

They typically give me a wide-eyed look of surprise and tell me, "Hold on, hold on. I wasn't ready." Then they proceed with a bumbling explanation of their book. Don't do this! If you don't practice, you will sound like this. Maybe not exactly like this, but close. There is no "hold on, hold on" or "I wasn't ready" when it comes to being live on-camera.

Try this exercise:

1. Write down your questions
2. Write down your answers
   a) Are the answers long?

      If they, are bullet point them into chunks of no more than two short sentences that get the point across that you are trying to make without all the fluff.
3. Look over this and go over the Q&A OUT LOUD. Read it the first few times out loud and then adjust as necessary depending on how it

sounds. Things look great on paper, but the way we talk is different than the way we write. Make sure you write it all out in a way that sounds good and is easy to discuss.

4. Once you've made your adjustments and like the way it sounds out loud, go over it often and in front of a mirror.
It's great to see your facial expressions when you talk about your book so that you are aware of how you might come across. I have an issue with this myself. When I am not actively aware of my facial expressions, I tend to frown... A LOT. It's usually because I am thinking or concentrating or interested in something, but it can come off as me looking angry. Be sure that you catch these things that might give people the wrong impression if you are on camera.

5. Record yourself
This will help you catch things that you miss in front of the mirror. Things like talking too quickly, saying um or like, looking down or around the room are things that you might not be able to catch in the mirror. Make sure to watch it with friends or family and ask for their honest opinion.

The above exercises will help you to walk into your interview confident and help you to drive the right messaging.

FIND THE RIGHT OUTFIT

This may seem trivial or like a no-brainer, but attire is a component in building your brand. A pantsuit sends a different message than a bright blouse and jeans. Whatever it is you decide to wear, make sure it is a true reflection of you and your book, and don't try to overplay the "author" role if it truly isn't you.

Stick with solid colors and clothing that don't have logos if you are on camera and lay off crazy patterns, because they can look weird on-camera. If you tend to accessorize a lot, make sure that it doesn't make a lot of noise because it can be picked up on mics. If you want to make a statement, now's the time, but make sure that it's the right statement that is true to you and your brand/book and make sure that visual statement doesn't interfere with your message about the book. Whatever it is that you pick out, make sure that you have it ready to wear, and in your closet. Authors have called me panicking last minute, because they can't find anything to wear for their on-camera interview. Be prepared. Picking something out ahead of time, before you book that interview, can help with getting your look just right and not having to scramble last minute for something that really shows who you are and brands you.

CHAPTER 17:
FINAL THOUGHTS

The field of Public Relations is growing in more ways than we can imagine. There is a constant flux of innovative campaigns that are not only changing the world but also changing perceptions. As we see more and more campaigns like these, we realize how influential the world of Public Relations really is. And as the influence grows in society, so do the roles.

Media is abundant. There is so much more that you have to compete with to garner attention, but there is also so much more that you can be a part of if you are prepared and approach it the right way. Authors now have a plethora of channels and mediums to showcase their books, many of these at no cost to them.

PR isn't easy, because if it were, then everyone would be doing it, but neither is writing a book. I am positive that if you have the discipline to write a book, then you definitely have the discipline to create and manage a stellar campaign for your book. Don't let your dream end once your book has been published because so much more magic lies within it for you to impart.

Share your love for writing and your talent with the world; you never know whose life you'll make an impact on.

I hope that this book has helped you get a clearer vision of what it takes for a successful PR campaign and given you the gumption and confidence to do it. Please always remember that if you have any questions, I'm always available to help. Best wishes on your PR adventure!

For more information about me, visit my company website at: www.DoGoodPRGroup.com.

For questions about the book or to connect with me, then email me at: www.DoGoodPRGroup.com/contact.

Keep up with me on all my social media for more insight, videos, free tutorials, information about upcoming writing and PR retreats and tons of other cool and fun stuff.

Facebook www.facebook.com/DoGoodPRGroup

Twitter @dogoodprgroup

Instagram @dogoodprgroup

ACKNOWLEDGMENTS

I would like to thank so many people who have helped and supported my writing and work. First, to my wonderful husband, thank you so much for all of the pep talks and hugs when I needed them most. Next, to all of my clients who inspire me and continue to amaze me, you make my job so much more meaningful. To my colleagues and friends who have helped not only with encouraging my writing, but also took the time to give me the feedback that I needed: Margaret Nice, Georgia Gidney, Lacey Ralston, and my wonderful editor Alan Passman, you guys rock! And finally to the two women who taught me how to be strong and savvy for others so that their voices and stories could be heard, my mother and grandmother.

ABOUT THE AUTHOR

Natalie Obando is the founder of Do Good Public Relations. She graduated from California State University, Long Beach with a BA in Journalism, an emphasis in Public Relations, and a minor concentration in Creative Writing. Natalie started working in the literary PR industry while in college and her love for books and PR transpired into the career of her dreams as a literary publicist.

In her off time, you can find her working with different animal rescue groups, walking her dogs on the beach, or combing through the shelves at her favorite book store or library. She also volunteers with organizations that help feed the homeless and help the working poor.

Beyond all the writing she does for the numerous campaigns she manages, she still finds time to work on her books and novel(s). She is passionate about writing, media, and making a difference.

For more information about her work, visit her website at: www.DoGoodPRGroup.com

www.ingramcontent.com/pod-product-compliance
Lightning Source LLC
LaVergne TN
LVHW050045090426
835510LV00043B/3022

* 9 7 8 0 9 9 7 1 2 9 6 0 1 *